Financial Independence Retire Early

Change Your Future One Simple Step at a Time

Michael McDonough

CM

Creative Media Enterprises

Copyright

Financial Independence Retire Early: Change Your Future One Simple Step at a Time

Preface

We are all after freedom in one way, shape or form. We want time to spend with our family, have a hobby, or to take time to learn a new language, even to live abroad. We don't want, "the man" breathing down our neck, and taking a bite out of our freedom. This book will teach the principals, guidelines and the pathway to achieve financial freedom, so you can retire early. Financial independence comes with just that, options. Options, to either quit your 9-5, start a company, travel, really, do what the hell you want.

My journey started after my spouse and I divorced, and I reviewed my income, assets, debt, that we had accumulated and realized there must be some other way. The American dream that I was living, started to sound like a sham to me. I had to dig in further. I was investing and saving, but what I ultimately discovered was I was spinning my wheels.

I'm almost embarrassed to say too, that I have been in the financial industry for nearly 16 years, and believed I governed my finances in the most astute way, so I thought. I had a good sized 401(k) and a savings account, that I believed, was plentiful. I felt secure in my job and was climbing the corporate ladder, and enjoyed my vacations, planned of course. I honestly thought this is what I should do. I was following "orders" was a good citizen, and believed this was the pathway for me. I was quite proud of my accomplishments and the amount I have saved and invested. Until I had a wakeup call, and discovered the financial independence movement.

I started to read about financial independence, now again, keep in mind, it was not a new topic for me, and I felt very well versed in financial matters, but I had a true moment of reflection and felt everything I was aiming for, was not in alignment with the ultimate objective for my long-term goals. I continued to research and accumulate knowledge, and realized I had to make changes, and major changes at that, if I wanted to free myself and change my future, financially speaking.

I started to implement several strategies, and as I was learning them, I began to see a difference. I started to cut back on non-essential items (that I thought I needed) and instead invested the savings into an index fund. Bit by bit, I changed the way I behaved with money, and began to gain a new perspective and relationship with it.

If I was so well versed, and it turns out, I wasn't at the time, just a soldier in essence, you may be in that same boat. Perhaps, you contribute 5% of your salary toward your 401(k) and believe you are right on target to retire at the ripe age of 65, which may be true, and believe you are on the targeted track for financial freedom; if so, this book is for you.

This book will challenge, inspire, be a wakeup call, and hopefully motivate you to take action, and massive action at that. The goal here is to change the trajectory of your financial matters so you can retire early, and benefit from financial freedom and independence.

I will provide the guidance and tools so you can live life on your terms, and not have to be stuck in the 9-5 grind, should you not want that path. All the information you need to be successful in this endeavor, is contained here in this book, with simple, easy to follow steps so you can get started today. I want everyone to know that financial independence is possible, with the steps and strategies we will lay out in this book, so you can change your future, one simple step at a time.

Michael

Introduction

W ould you like to make steps today, so you can change your financial future and live life on your own terms?

Do you want to be free from your 9-5 so you can start a business, a hobby, or travel the world? Are you looking to exit your corporate job as soon as possible?

Do you want to build a life, that provides for financial freedom, giving you the luxury to be able to retire early with passive income streams, so you can do what you want?

Many of us think that retiring by the time we are 30, 40, or 50 is unattainable due to massive debt, corporate restructuring, or because you don't have the time to dedicate into a strong financial education on financial independence. The notion of retiring early has become merely a dream in the far distance future that does not appear to be a reality in the present day.

Or, maybe you are like me, who I thought I had my financial matters in order, until I had a wake-up call. I was deplored when I discovered I was spinning my wheels, and was not investing as much as I should be. I was concerned with other matters, and not focusing on my financial future.

Maybe I am speaking to you, in that you feel that you have your financial matters in order, and are doing everything right, but realize you are not getting ahead as much as you hope. This movement of Financial Independence, so you can retire early, changed the way I thought and my attitude toward money, and

I hope it has an impact on your financial mindset so your future self can reap the benefits of financial independence and the freedom that comes with it.

Financial Independence, Retire Early, (or F.I.R.E.), is a lifestyle movement that aims to achieve financial independence and early retirement. Those who aim to achieve F.I.R.E. deliberately optimize their saving rate by finding ways to raise their income and to reduce costs. The main objective is to accumulate assets until passive income generates enough money in perpetuity to offset the cost of living. The main principle is that the higher your salary, comparatively low expenditures coupled with radical investing, the sooner you will be able to gain financial freedom.

Many proponents of the F.I.R.E. movement propose the 4 percent rule as a guideline, stemmed from the Trinity Study, thus setting a target of at least 25 times the estimated annual living expenses. Upon achieving financial independence, paid work becomes optional, allowing for retirement from traditional work decades earlier than the standard retirement age (Kagan, 2020).

This movement of Financial Independence with the ability to retire early has taken off in the past couple decades. This movement, consists of investing in passive income sources, and wild frugality, so you can live a life on your terms.

Many are changing daily habits and embracing the pathway to financial independence. Financial independence will allow for life on your terms, not relying on your 9-5, so you can be free from the burden of working for another in perpetuity.

Are you ready to change your financial future? Are you ready to make small, simple changes today and get started on your path to financial independence?

We are going to dive in to the strategies so you can change the trajectory of your financial future. The process will not happen overnight. This is not a quick fix and there are no guarantees for a certain outcome as financial matters do contain risk. This will, however, provide tools, and strategies, which others have used successfully, to grow their wealth over time. This is not a get rich quick book.

Investing and creating passive income is a strategy to be held over the long haul, years, decades. You will not be rich tomorrow after reading this book; what you will have is the skills and tips, like I needed, to get you from A to B, and to move you further down the pathway than where you are today. This book is a wakeup call to review your financial matters, come to terms with your present day, and to get a plan for financial independence, creating it one simple step at a time.

Here is a synopsis of what we will cover and what you will learn in this book:

- Why People are Embracing the Financial Independence Lifestyle Movement, Rapidly and Heavily Investing in Passive Income Sources

- 23 Practical Steps to Create Wealth with Clearly Defined Steps to so you Can Easily Get on Board with the FIRE Movement

- How to Get Started with Investments so you Can Generate Wealth and Change your Financial Future

- How to Calculate your Retirement Date so you Can Taste your Future and Start to Make Retirement Plans

- How to Create Passive Income with the BRRRR Approach to Real Estate Investing so you Can Diversify your Assets

- The Magic of Compound Interest so you can See your Investments Grow

- The Importance of our Mindset and how it Impacts our

Ability to Generate Wealth

- How to Overcome Setbacks and Challenges so that you Can Quickly Gain Momentum

- The Impact of Embracing a Frugal Mentality so you Can Boost your Portfolio Forward and see the Day of Financial Independence

- How to Get out of the Rat Race so you Can Enjoy your Life and Live It on your Own Terms

- 9 Side Hustles to Start Today to Propel you Forward in the Journey Faster

- And more...

Can you picture yourself getting up, having your morning cup of coffee, and not having to report in to your boss?

Would you love to be present more with your family and spend more time with them?

Do you want to accumulate wealth by making small steps and changes today?

Are you looking to secure your financial future in uncertain times?

Maybe you are looking to get out of the rat race, and do not wish to work for 30 or 40 years for a corporate giant, before you can rest and do what you want.

Is there a business idea that you would love to dedicate your time, energy and resources to but do not have time to do so, because your 9-5 is demanding your time – even on the weekends?

Let's go, your future is waiting...

Contents

Chapter One

Financial Independence

"Financial fitness is not a pipe dream or a state of mind. It's a reality if you are willing to pursue it and embrace it." Will Robinson

F inancial Independence Retire Early, (or F.I.R.E.), is not a new discovery, the concept has been around for some time; however, it has become a new recent trend stemmed from various factors. Many are moving toward the F.I.R.E. philosophy due to not wanting to "work for the man" for 30 or 40 years in a job that does not provide for satisfaction. Others are concerned with being bored or complacent in a job, or a stuck in a career that is less than desirable.

Financial independence is the situation of having enough income (from investments, passive income sources, real estate, etc.) to pay for one's acceptable living expenses for the rest of one's life without needing to depend on formal employment. The core path to achieving financial independence focuses on maximizing one's savings rate by reducing expenses with high incomes.

The philosophy behind F.I.R.E. recently re-emerged in the USA, and some of its ideas were first published in a book called "Your Money or Your Life," in 1992, written by Vicki Robin and Jon Domínguez (Maroon, 2020). They propagated the idea of living frugally and gaining investment income to gain financial freedom early in life.

Financial freedom would mean the right to live more or less as one wishes within acceptable limits. It may not mean the absolute freedom never to work another day - but this should mean the freedom to leave a poor job, go back to school, or start up a company without a big sacrifice. Also, financial stability should involve having the means to cope with the ups and downs of life without squandering, sacrificing, or falling deeply into debt.

The F.I.R.E. movement also adheres to the conventional ideas of gaining financial independence and establishing a savings corpus, but withdraws much earlier in existence, likely in the 40's or 30's, which is decades before the normal retirement age.

Many ultimately choose to aim toward F.I.R.E, because they want to live life on their terms. Many want to travel and experience the world, see new places and not be held down by corporate obligations or having to earn their next paycheck. Corporate restructuring is a fear for many, especially due to recent events, and several are changing their mindset and embracing F.I.R.E. as soon as they hear about it.

Maybe you have seen your parents work for a company for decades, and you do not want to follow suit. You want to experience life, have financial freedom, and have the means to make independent decisions and not have someone else be in charge of your future.

Apart from the early retirement dimension, the F.I.R.E. philosophy varies in more than one way from traditional methods. For example, when you think about financial planning, you're still trying to improve your current lifestyle. Still, F.I.R.E.'s philosophy will allow you to maintain a lifestyle even after retirement to cover your monthly expenses in most situations.

Financial Independence Retire Early may be a monetary movement characterized by frugality and minimalism and outrageous reserve funds and ventures. By saving up to 70% of yearly salary, F.I.R.E. proponents shall retire early and live off little withdrawals from amassed reserves (Hogan, 2020).

What is F.I.R.E?

Financial Independence, Retire Early is a movement that does not necessarily mean snorkeling, golfing, or traveling the world, though they are things you may wish to do once achieved. It's about freedom. Freedom to live your life the way you want with sustainability. It means getting to the place in your life where you don't have to work a corporate job if you don't want to. You can start a business, go back to part-time work, or you might just stop working and travel, the choice and the option is yours.

Many proponents of the F.I.R.E. movement propose the 4 percent rule as a guideline, thus setting a target of at least 25 times the estimated annual living expenses, based upon the Trinity Study (more on this later). When financial independence is achieved, work in the traditional sense, as in the 9-5, is now optional, which allows you to retire early earlier than the anticipated age of 59 ½.

Financial Independence, Retire Early is also be a movement dedicated to an establishment of extraordinary reserve funds that allows proponents to resign far before customary spending plans and retirement plans would permit. By devoting up to 70% of pay to investment, adherents of the movement may, within the end of the day, have the decision to retire from their occupations and live exclusively off little withdrawals from their portfolio's decades before the regular retirement age.

F.I.R.E. isn't a sure-FIRE plan, with it comes with *living intentionally with less by choice* and adhering to and standards of frugality (though all do not choose to live frugally) with limiting many of the common pleasures of the standard of life, for a time, to achieve the plan. This lifestyle would need to be thought of and embraced with a certain level of comfort and due diligence.

Retirement has a different meaning from those who are striving toward the F.I.R.E. Movement; traditionally, our retirement age is 65. Adherents to the F.I.R.E movement, generally wish to retire as early as possible, much earlier than 65 (or 59 ½), usually in their 40's, 30's, and sometimes even in their 20's.

Financial independence is the fact of being in total financial autonomy. The capital or the income is greater than the family's expenses and this without having to work or deprive yourself of certain things. Financial independence can be obtained through different investments such as the stock market, real estate investments, owning your own business, passive income, in addition to a salary etc. But it is above all, a situation which requires flawless accounting. Chance has no place. The best time to start putting your plan into action is right now. The sooner the better. The time is now.

What do people really want? Why do many people want to retire early? Do they want to sit on a beach, play golf or travel? Many do wish to do this, but for a time, but let's take a look at the real motive for financial independence.

Freedom and Time

People don't want more money necessarily, they want more freedom: spending time with family and friends, traveling more, and doing whatever they want. In most cases, you don't have to be a millionaire to do what you love. What you really need is enough money to maintain the lifestyle you want - this state is called financial independence. The meaning of financial independence or financial freedom can be summed up in one sentence: living off your income without having to work for a salary.

Financial independence occurs when you have sufficient personal wealth to maintain your current spending habits throughout your life without needing to earn more money. You may choose to work for other reasons, such as passion or intent, but you no longer need to have a job to fund your lifestyle.

For financially independent people, their assets generate more income than their expenses. For example, if the annual expenses of a person are $30,000 per year and dividend income from stocks totals $40,000 per year, while having more money in other assets such as real estate, in this circumstance, this person is financially independent.

To be financially independent is NOT TO BE OBLIGED to get up in the morning and go to work to pay your bills. So, financial independence means having alternative / passive income (real estate, business creation, stock market) which occurs every month without you trading your time for it, and these must be able to cover your needs. You will no longer have to get up in the morning and do a job that pisses you off in order to pay your bills.

Many are seeking this freedom so they can spend their time any way they please. In order to have more time, many are seeking to get out of the rat race. What is this rat race?

The concept of the "Rat Race" is an image used by Robert Kiyosaki, an entrepreneur born in Hawaii in 1947, who wrote "Rich Dad, Poor Dad". In his book, Kiyosaki, compares the human being to a laboratory rat circling around in his wheel or in his labyrinth. The concept criticized is that man misses his life according to the pattern of functioning most widespread in our modern societies. He exchanges his time for a salary to pay his credits, his bills, his taxes, and when he has the need, to buy superfluous goods or services (Kiyosaki & Lechter, 1997). Is this you? Are you exchanging your time for money with the hopes and thoughts to get ahead, so one day you can be free?

How do you know if you are in the "Rat Race?"

We are in the "Rat Race" when we work in order to receive a salary in order to support our lifestyle. As soon as you say: "In my current job, I will work in order to receive a salary in order to support my lifestyle", you are in the rat race. You will tell me that under these conditions, 99% of people are in the "Rat Race?" Well, yes. Suddenly you are probably in it, as I have been for many years without even realizing it.

Is that bad? No, if you are completely fulfilled, have no additional financial needs, and have time to do whatever it is you love to do. While that's okay, many find it to not be fulfilling and feel stuck in this Rat Race. It is even a question of survival when one tries to escape it.

How Can you Get Out of the "Rat Race?"

Leaving the "Rat Race" is not done by putting everything in your life as we can see in certain stories, "they sold their house, quit their job and went around the world." No, getting out of the "Rat Race" is a goal you set for yourself, with a plan of action to get there. Then, it's going to take time, which is why you need to act as soon as possible and not just think about it.

First, let's discuss the concept of active income and passive income. You have an active income when you have to spend the time to generate it, while as passive income is generated automatically without the need to devote time to it. If you earn your income from work then you have active income, conversely if you have financial investments or real estate that you rent out you have passive income.

When passive income is greater than your active income, you can choose to leave the "rat race" if you so please, since the income you derive from passive source(s) covers the active.

First you need to start by getting a plan together. If you do not make a plan, a financial plan for your future, a plan will be created by default and it will be lackluster. In fact, you may be on the default plan right now and not even know it.

If you live your life without a financial plan in order, one that you have, one that you have deliberately and carefully crafted, I guarantee there will be someone in your life, who will dictate what they feel is the plan and you. If this has occurred and you are on the default plan, you are a *responder* to the plan, instead of creating it.

Without a financial plan, there will be someone else will be happy to take care of your financial future for you: your boss (will ask for extended hours to show involvement); your spouse (will want more financial means to buy the latest Louboutins); your parents (will choose the ideal job for you according to their own criteria); your financial advisor (who may love the opportunity to make money off your assets, and who does watch your funds as carefully as you might come to expect, not to mention the fees); your children (will claim a minimum 4 hotel vacations to impress friends on Facebook) and; the state (which through ever greater interventionism will tell you that it knows better than you, on how to use your money) and will always ask for more. You must take back control of your life and must not place the definition of the quality in the hands of another well-meaning (or not) person. There is a future waiting. The future has F.I.R.E. written all over it. By what type of F.I.R.E.?

It almost doesn't matter what type of F.I.R.E., as FIRE is FIRE, but there are variances in the way one achieves FIRE as well as the way one lives, while in FIRE. What is common between these variances, is they have all obtained a level of financial independence and have created the lifestyle they want, intentionally.

Variation of F.I.R.E.

Inside the growing movement are several styles that direct the way enthusiasts are capable and prepared to keep:

- Fat F.I.R.E.: usually high-income earners (lawyers, doctors, engineers) that may choose not to live frugally. They may entertain "living large", but they have the funds, savings and investment to do so.

- Lean F.I.R.E.: alludes to severe adherence to moderate living with healthy reserve funds, requiring an undeniably more limited way of life.

- Barista F.I.R.E.: alludes to adherents who have stopped their conventional 9-to-5 occupation yet, at an equivalent time, may have a part-time employment to offset expenses which may disintegrate their retirement.

- Coast F.I.R.E.: additionally, it applies to adherents that typically began to invest at a very young age. They may be able to stop contributing to investment funds and still be able to retire.

You can really pick any form of F.I.R.E., but it will boil down to the level of income vs. assets as it relates to your current expenditures. We don't have to get hung up on a particular F.I.R.E. type, but it's good to know there are levels. It's like getting the gold star vs. the silver or bronze. Bronze may be okay for many on the pathway to financial independence.

Too, you may be starting your journey in your 30's or 40's or even later. The great thing about the F.I.R.E. journey is you are not on a race with others. The goal is really up to you. You set the pace and the standard by which you will choose to live. There is no one out there with a F.I.R.E. measuring stick, and there is no one who even may encourage you to keep on with this passion.

Yes, that's right, the pathway to F.I.R.E., is independent and often self-motivated. You are your own biggest hero. No one may congratulate you when your stock portfolio hits a milestone. No one may tell you, you are awesome, when you purchase your third investment home. No one may tell you that you are fantastic, when you max out your 401 (k), this year, and your spouse's along with your Roth IRA's. There are no cheerleaders and oftentimes many tell you to go back to the way you were before the F.I.R.E. movement.

The cheerleaders have gone silent and your friends do not understand why you will not meet up with them on their next trip to Mexico. You feel you are being laughed at, even mocked, by close friends and some family, who are aware of your F.I.R.E. journey. They may be on the default plan and can't understand why you have gone mad investing so heavily into passive income streams. You are investing so heavily that they tell you to calm down, they remind you of the risk associated with investing and they feel their mission is to warn you, to help you see things from a different, even healthy financial perspective, to even "shed light" for you.

Let's get it out of the way here and early. There will be many, including close friends and family that will not approve of you going hog wild into your new F.I.R.E. journey. They will come up with all sorts of reasons why you are making a grave error and you do not know what you are doing. You will hear all the excuses. Choose who you want to let them know of your F.I.R .E., journey, but be prepared for backlash with an unsupportive and judgmental crowd who won't clap for you. Yes, there will be some who will encourage you, but oftentimes, it's few and far between. This is why it's essential to be self-motivating with a clear goal, and a vision, with a well-thought-out plan. The plan will provide guidance until the goal is met, whether its Fat F.I.R.E, Barista F.I.R.E. or you just coasted your way into F.I.R.E.

When you have hit F.I.R.E, you have reached the destination, which is at least 25 times your annual spend. And once you have this figure, if you withdraw at a rate of around 4 percent a year (some say 3.5 percent, others say 3 percent, and some even more recently are now saying 5 percent), you can retire should you choose to do so. Many continue on, even once they have reached F.I.R.E, to fatten up and reach Fat F.I.R.E. Why are so many seeking financial independence?

Life Expectancy is Increasing

The generation of our parents was told that you had to work to earn a living, that it was the natural order of things. Most of us have parents who are exhausted by their jobs, and who suffer from work-related illness and have high-stress levels. Maybe you have witnessed someone burn-out in their career or have become complacent with loss of ambition.

We know what's important in life: our time and freedom. The race to accumulate wealth seems futile, as we will not take our cars, jewelry, and other gadgets to the grave. On the other hand, we finally realize that our time is limited and must make the best use of our time and resources. While we cannot take anything with us to the grave, we can choose how we life our life with the time we do have. We can make decisions today that will have a lasting impact on our future and maybe even change the financial trajectory for generations to come. There is no crime in freedom. Just because the generations prior to us, worked one way, we can learn a new way, with a different outcome with obtaining our freedom one day sooner than yesterday.

Statistics show Americans are living longer. This means time spent in retirement is increasing. Life expectancy is 78.7 for the total U.S. population for 2018. For males, it is 76.2 while for females it is 81.2 (Xu et al., 2020). Life expectancy is increasing. We have no choice but to work longer to guarantee a decent level of retirement; however, some understand it differently in the F.I.R.E movement. This F.I.R.E. movement defends the principle of saving abundantly and investing wisely so you can stop working, or work less.

Is financial independence really achievable?

Success Story - Mr. Money Mustache

Mr. Money Mustache, has a popular blog on how he, Peter Adeney, achieved Financial Independence, and retired from his corporate career at age 30. In fact, it wasn't just he alone who retired early, but his wife did. Behind Mr. Mustache's nickname, we find a Canadian in his forties now who, was a computer engineer, like his wife. According to his own words, their salaries were those of "basic high-tech employees."

From his first salary he sets aside: $5,000 the first year, and $25,000 the following year. He meets his future wife, also an engineer. When their friends or colleagues skyrocket their salaries and take trips, eat out in restaurants, get fancy new cars, indulge in the latest luxury brands, they save, and they save and invest heavily. They saved upward of 70% each month. They did their math. They ran the numbers. They increased their investments exponentially and learned to live on less. They embraced frugality and now have a different life. You see, they wanted to be around for their children, being physically present. They wanted to have time to do what they wanted, and be free.

By the time Mr. Money Mustache was 30, he was retired. They had over $500,000 set aside, and they had a paid for house which was worth approximately $180,000. They quit and gave up the rat race at an age many would scoff at. Now, Adeney, lives in Colorado, spending $25,000 a year, at the time for three. The couple managed to save around two-thirds of their income, invested it and lived frugally.

Adeney had also undertaken renovations to a home purchased while working. So, he rented it out and bought a much cheaper one. This property earns him $25,000 in rent net of tax per year, roughly what his household spends each year. Because Adeney still leads a very modest life and continues to save, the dividends earned by money placed in market indexed funds are always reinvested. At the time, it was around $12,000 per year (Adeney, 2019).

It's absolutely possible to retire early with financial means to live and do as you please. The sooner you start to invest, the sooner your day of freedom approaches. By making choices, which add up over time, pun intended, you can change your financial future.

What is the right method to attain financial independence? Is there just one way?

The Right Method

There are many methods to achieve financial independence, let's start with some of the basics. It will depend mainly on what and how you want to live in retirement. Here are the steps that will allow for financial independence and early retirement:

Put Money Aside

Save and then spend what is left and not the other way around. The higher the percentage of savings compared to your salary, the faster you will have significant assets to be financially independent or allow you to have a temporary retirement during your career. You may wish to take a personal hiatus from your corporate professional for a time to unwind, find a new career, or even try to develop a personal project or business undertaking that is close to your heart.

In order to put as much aside, and if you have a considerable amount of debt, I strongly advise you to liquidate all your consumer debts (credit card, consumer loan, car loan). Without this first move, you will not be able to save enough. The less debt you have, the more you can save and invest.

Live Below Your Means

Keep a tight budget on your expenses, even if you earn a good living. Why waste money by buying things you really don't need?

If you earn a good living, and buy a bigger home because you just got a raise and you claim you can afford it, it may be the very thing that is setting you back from achieving financial independence. Instead of upgrading your life, when your income grows, live below your means, and as far below it as you can stand it. Typically, those who live in smaller houses have less maintenance need less furniture and "stuff" to fill all the rooms. Having less space to store all the things that we buy on impulse too, can reduce the physical clutter and even help to bring about a focused mindset.

Evaluate if you really need something before making a purchase. Many times, we are so used to showing the credit card for a new trendy item without thinking of how it impacts our financial future. Many times, we are living in the moment and we lose sight of our financial future and how certain items and "needs" are not really needs at all. Let's keep it real, we may have become used to the rush of endorphins a purchase provides. Too, we may be trying to impress our friends or neighbors. Break the pattern of over-consuming as it will only set you back from your target, and cut back. Reduce the need to buy the latest gadget (which they claim you absolutely need) which will probably just sit around collecting dust. Think of ways to decrease your grocery bill. Buy less meat, which is typically expensive, and see if there are alternatives that you enjoy just as much. Challenge yourself to see how frugal and with a minimalist mindset you can handle, even for a time.

Choose the Right Place to Live

The more you live in the big "trendy" cities, the more difficult it will be to achieve this financial independence. Think about moving to a different location, one that has a lower cost of living. Right now, during this global pandemic, many people are relocating to a different part of the country. Many are also making moves internationally as their job no longer requires them to go into the office every day. Now, more than ever before, there are options to consider. Think if relocating is right for you.

Calculate your assets and your FI Number

Add up the funds from all your bank accounts, real estate investments, stock market and others. Forget about cars, arts or luxury items; they do not produce cash flows, their liquidity is nonexistent, or they devalue over time. From all these assets you must deduct all your debts. This will give you what is called your net assets. Calculating your net assets will help you see where you are today so you can make a plan to adjust accordingly.

To calculate your Financial Independence Number, you will need to know your annual expenses. Take your annual expenses and multiply by 25, for the 4% rule. If you need $50K per year to live, for example, you will need investments of $1,250.000 ($50,000 × 25). Pause and figure out the amount you need to retire. This is your FI Number (Kagan, 2020). With your FI number, you now know what is your magic number to strive for. The goal is to hit this number as soon as possible. This is the beginning of the financial journey.

Next, we will explore our mindset. Do you believe having a clear focus will help to achieve financial independence? Let's take a look.

Chapter Two

Mindset

"A strong, positive self-image is the best possible preparation for success." Joyce Brothers

F inancial independence doesn't come just because people ask for it, or because they decide they want it. It is not happenstance. Our bank accounts are not going to grow just because we want it to. We will not own real estate simply because, we think it's a good idea. The pathway to financial independence takes time. It takes careful planning and execution. It takes reevaluating decisions from time to time. If your plan is to own real estate, you will have to make it a priority.

If your plan is to be financially free, it has to drive you. When we decide we want to be financially independent, we choose to allow this philosophy to be interwoven into all areas of life. This decision, may be one of the biggest decisions in your life. It may change everything. It may change the way you view relationships; it may change where you choose to live, it may change the idea of what car you drive and the friends you have. It may change your hobbies, all of it. So beware, this book may just change our life. Financial independence doesn't happen without cause, without planning and without having the proper mindset.

The pathway to financial independence is also a choice, and a personal one at that. I wish it would be easy to say that financial matters are not personal, yet that wouldn't be true. In fact, financial matters are very personal, our finances for the most part, dictate what we do with our time. The choice to follow this pathway, is a personal one, and it may impact other decisions in your life and honestly, it should. But again, no one will make this choice for you. It comes from within, seeing the big picture, and realizing the goal is attainable.

Our mind is one of the strongest tools we have at our disposal. Before we venture forward on the path to financial independence, we have to be certain our mind is in the right place. When our mind is focused on this journey, we increase our chance of success. Having the right mindset will help us overcome tough times or when we are faced with struggles and challenges. The path to financial freedom, is not an all-uphill battle with victory after victory. It's filled with ups and downs, just like the stock market, so we have to mentally prepare ourself now for it. With a strong mindset, we can overcome obstacles.

As we can see, not only do we have to have a formal plan for financial independence, but the process of obtaining it, may take some grit from time to time. Financial independence will require determination and resilience coupled with an astute mindset. Steve Maraboli says, "Once your mindset changes, everything on the outside will change along with it." (Maraboli, 2019) It's essential to have our mind in the right place as we are on the financial independence journey.

Grit, determination and resilience is needed to cross the finish line – this is our mindset and it's has the biggest impact on whether we will be financially free in time. As we said earlier, financial freedom and independence, does not happen overnight. There is no secret pill to being financially independent, but it will take a mindset that is set on achieving this goal. What is your mind telling you today? Are you ready to move forward on this journey? Let's take a look at the two types of mindsets.

There are two types of mindsets. One is the fixed mindset and the other is a growth mindset. A fixed mindset is where you believe that you cannot change. You believe what you believe and have no plans for growth, learning new perspectives, different ways of thinking, or adapting to new processes. You are firm and unmovable. The growth mindset, on the other hand, means that you are open to new opportunities, new perspectives, options, and are willing to learn from past mistakes. Mistakes are viewed optimally as learning opportunities and the mind has shifted into a state of perpetual growth.

One of my good friends often tells me that brain surgeons did not come out of the womb knowing how to perform surgery. They were taught. I always appreciated his words of encouragement, and it's so true. We are truly on an endless journey of not only self-discovery, but we are constantly in a state of learning and progressing, no matter our age. It has also been said, that "shifting to a growth mindset will allow us to live with less stress and to achieve a greater level of success" (Dweck, 2016). I truly believe this as well, when we live with a growth mindset, we can do more, and accomplish much more than we feel we can on the onset. Inhabiting a growth mindset will help to propel us to able to reach our goal. Financial independence is on the way, can you taste it?

The journey to financial independence takes years, decades to achieve, but our mindset is key. It will help us to hover around obstacles, life events, market conditions, to keep pushing toward our goal. It's the hidden strength from within. It's the fire on our path, no pun intended. It's the light on our journey and keeps us moving forward one step at a time, day by day, month by month, and year by year. We have to get our mindset in order and continue in the growth mindset. Take the time right now to think about what type of mindset you have. Do you have a growth mindset, or a fixed mindset?

Once we have our mind in order, we can take the next step to evaluate our needs vs. wants. Once we learn the true difference, we will make clearer decisions on our path to financial freedom.

Needs Vs. Wants

Once our mindset has been established, this will set the foundation to which we can explore other areas in our life. It's time to review our needs vs. wants. Many people feel they need a certain thing, or need to do a certain task, but it's really a want or a desire they feel strongly toward. There is a fine line between these two concepts.

A need is the absolute requirement for life, think food, water, and shelter. Desire or a want, is something that will make life more comfortable and enjoyable. For example, I need to drink to quench my thirst, but if I drink a fruit juice rather than water, it is about desire not need. There is a necessity on the one hand vs. a desire on the other. This concept gets confused often. Too, we may justify a desire as a need.

When we think about needs vs. wants within the realm of financial independence, we need to be able to separate true needs from wants. The wants may be something we either cut back on for a time, or we may choose to keep them in our life due to the comfort and ease of life they bring. Seeing items from these two perspectives, helps us to propel our growth mindset so we can clearly differentiate our needs vs. wants.

Financial independence *desires* may include budgeting for travel or a gym membership, dining out, etc. Desires are dependent on collective perspectives and cultural influences. It is desire that opens up a space of freedom; it is a luxury that cannot be experienced by those whose basic needs have not been met. We are linked to the idea of luxury not to the necessary.

Desires are not wrong, it's what propels us and causes us to use our growth mindset to achieve our goals. Desires pushes us to be greater, to accomplish more, to withstand hard times and struggles to get to our destination. We see our future tangibly and *desire* will help us get there. Desire is the driving force and the wind that blows through our hair. If it was just about meeting needs, we wouldn't need to work so damn hard. Desire involves consciousness, choice, imagination, and progression. To *desire* is to strive for an object, that as I imagine it, is a promise of pleasure. To desire is to be human and seek greater purpose.

The drive to becoming financially free and independent of working the 9-5 and to be able to retire early, takes this growth mindset, coupled with desire, and is the fuel for a different outcome for your life. It is the basic undertone and sets the pace for financial independence.

Do you dream of changing your life? Do you dream of a greater future for yourself and for your family? Do you want to be financially free; do you want to get F.I.R.E.'d? What does it take to get F.I.R.E.'d?

Lifestyle Change

Let's keep it real, it's hard to make changes. It's hard to go on a whole new trajectory at a moment's notice. What I have come to learn, is many who have discovered the F.I.R.E. movement have done just that. They have shifted their mindset almost instantly.

But, is it easy? Will it take work? Will it happen in just one day? Changing our mindset will take time.

Many, once they have discovered this movement have taken right off never to look back. The mental shift occurred almost instantly as they saw the big picture and it all made sense. As said earlier, the desire for financial independence may just change everything – from your mind, to your habits, to your job. Many clearly saw their future financial lives on the table, and created momentum from that point forward.

Momentum is a key ingredient to bring financial independence to fruition. Momentum brings the desire to paper and is filled with action. Action will further bring our goals together, so much so, we will start to taste it. To fuel this momentum, you have got to really know what you want. Really. Nail it down. Write it on the fridge. Post it on the bathroom wall. When you eat rice and beans for dinner, I want you to feel your goals in your hands, and I want you to taste the momentum, some say its sweet and addictive like sugar.

For momentum to take off, you have got to really know what you want. What are you focusing on? What are you complaining about? Are you complaining about never having enough money? Your terrible job? The lack of funds in your 401(k)? Take note of where your attention is currently. What is on your mind right now? Are you focusing on the negative, things you don't have or where you want to be? Are you downcast, and stuck in your current pattern of thought?

If you are likely in the majority of people who claim to be dissatisfied with their current lifestyle, or career – you are not alone. It has been reported that nearly up to 70 percent of employees are actively disengaged at work (Nordstrom, 2018). Their mind is elsewhere. When we are on the journey toward financial independence, we need to regain our perspective and get engaged in life. We have got to take a mental stand for ourself and what we want. This starts right now.

Don't be like the majority of people who are more likely to complain and talk about what they don't have, living unfocused lives filled with desperation, and living for the weekend. How many times have you heard someone say, "Yeah, it's Friday," Many people love to complain at the water cooler but fear making a change - a lasting change that will have a great impact. They would rather vent it with their friends, spouse, and reinforces a way of thinking every time it's discussed.

When we are on the pathway to financial independence, we have to take a mental stand to transform our way of thinking and mindset to create what we want. It's a shift that goes deep. When we focus on the negative, we are re-creating these experiences over and over again. The pathway to financial freedom does not make time for this, and the fear that is associated with complaining and negative thinking, has no place. We must

push past this to get ahead. If you fall in this boat of negative thinking patterns, you have got to push past this. Use the
negative from whatever circumstance to propel you to financial
independence. If you are upset with your current job situation,
let your discomfort fuel you to make a change.

The less we concentrate on the negative, the less of a sting
it will carry, and the weight from the situation will no longer
weight us down. We have to literally choose to not allow it
to impact us any further. When the negative thought or a
complaining mentality comes, mentally shift into other things.
Make a transition to see it for what it is, but to see what we can
learn from the struggle, not to complain just to complain. Move
the complaining attitude toward progression.

Start by becoming aware of what you lack and from there,
formulate precisely what you want. Think of your FI number.
This will give yourself a direction to follow (not just something
to avoid). Those who manage to change, have given themselves
a precise and well-defined goal, which inspires them and carries
them forward.

Deciding what you want takes you forward. If you tell your mind
the direction you want it to go, then it will act as a steering
system and work for you. When you give it the destination to
avoid, it also works to get you where you don't want to go,
especially if your attention is there. Choose now, your path and
allow yourself to make the needed changes in thinking which
will impact performance.

Next, get to know yourself so well that your desired mindset
change corresponds to your value of financial freedom. It will be
easier if, before even starting to change your life, you firmly base
the decisions you are about to make on your values. Know what
your weak spots are, and where you may be challenged to spend
money unnecessarily, for example. It is therefore important to
identify them, that your choices do not put you in contradiction
with your objectives.

When we make these changes to achieve financial freedom and independence, we may run into some roadblocks. For instance, you may uncover, you like to purchase things online in excess. Maybe you are addicted to shopping on Amazon. You like the simple 1-click purchase option as it makes life so easy. In a couple days, a nice box shows up at the door without having to leave the house. The pathway to financial independence will also uncover some habits that we may have become accustomed. We may discover we have an addiction to shopping, or a mentality to have a nicer car than our neighbors or cousin. Living without certain things or performing certain actions may surface uncomfortable feelings. This is going to have to be decided upon. If you want to really be free from your 9-5, you are going to have to make choices you haven't made in a while. Log out of Amazon, and stop buying things you don't need on eBay.

Mind if I go a bit deeper for a moment? You may connect the items you have purchased with your inherent value as a person. You may think you deserve the items as you work hard for them. While that is true, realize that your value as a human is not measure by the toys, he /she accumulates. Your value is much more than stuff, or how early you retire for that matter.

Things do not dictate value in a person's life. When these feelings of inadequacy surface and it's connected to things, take time to evaluate your thoughts to hear reason and truth in the situation and move forward when ready. The journey to financial independence is wide and it's not always about saving as much money as possible, it goes "below the surface" and in a healthy way we are able to address issues and personal habits to have a better future.

When we make changes to our personal spending habits, either cutting back or having less, as our needs are less, we may feel a sense of grieving. We may not directly understand it as grieving, but we may be feeling a sense of loss. We may be used to a dopamine hit when we purchase an item, for example, and when we purchase less, we have a feeling that something is off. According to Ruth Engs from Indiana University, some people develop shopping addictions. The brain releases endorphins and dopamine. Engs claims that up to 15 percent of the population may have a shopping addiction (Hatfield, 2020). As lifestyle changes are made, and new habits are formed, it's okay to grieve prior habits. It takes time to adjust to a new mentality.

Letting go may seem simple at first glance, but it isn't always. Making changes that will impact your financial future may be challenging at first and that is okay. Make small changes gradually which may involve giving up and grieving perceived loss, these can be construed as gains prospectively. Know that your resistance to change is commensurate with your grief, as is the importance to identify it to progress forward. Any change carries with it its share of emotions. While some of them energize us, others can cause regression for a time. We must learn to dismantle the emotions that prevent us from progressing.

Lastly, let's take note of our surroundings. It's great to be around like-minded people. When we surround ourself with people on the same pathway, or those who are far ahead of us, it will encourage us further to our destination. It helps to know that we are on the right path, and that others are on the same journey. I implore you to surround yourself with others who are on the same journey. You can be a support system for them, and they for you – not to mention, there is usually someone who may push us past a certain level. We all need a push from time to time.

Once we have our mindset and momentum in check and we are moving forward, next we will focus in like a laser to bring our journey toward financial independence together.

Laser Focused

Do you want to be financially independent? Is the passion for freedom burning in your heart? Do you want to focus in on this task even more?

Mastering the skill of concentrating like a laser, will push our momentum forward exponentially. A laser sees no distraction, it's focused, determined and carries the power of momentum. It's the defining tool to generate sustainable wealth to last for decades, so we can retire at leisure, early if we so choose to do so. If you cannot master the skill of being laser focused, you may find yourself, "off the beaten path" and get sidetracked.

A laser is a system that uses crystals or special gases to generate a single-color light. The main word, is a single-color light, not a multi-color light. Much like a laser, you need to pull all your energy into becoming focused like a laser, toward the pursuit of financial independence. Concentrate on this mission intentionally.

What is the best way to focus?

The advice of Steve Jobs is to learn to say "No." Jobs is quoted, "People think focus means saying yes to the thing you've got to focus on. But that's not what it means at all. It means saying no to the hundred other good ideas that there are." (Jobs, 2016) Focusing means less speaking, more action. It means less time on social media. It means saying "No," to the hundred other distractions that call for our attention. Maintaining a laser concentration is about saying no to unnecessary data and acting on the knowledge that you already have. Get comfortable with your new favorite word.

The road to financial independence has characteristics of delayed gratification. It's like going on a diet, or when we want to change our eating habits. Instead of eating fast food and/or processed foods, we have to say, "No" to those certain foods and adapt a change in behavior and mental shift to making healthier food choices. It's delayed gratification. We put something off (or many things off for a time), to achieve freedom financially and a healthier diet. It's time to go on a financial diet. Delay the items you don't need, to pave the way for a better financial future.

Delayed gratification also comes into play if we are training to run a marathon, or just get fit again. We are delaying sitting on our couch, and even things that bring us joy, to obtain the goal. The path to financial independence is a vision, and a mission. Some changes will take place slowly, and bit by bit, we progress and get stronger, leaner and more focused. When we see evidence of success (saving a ton of money and our stock portfolio booming), it encourages us to keep going and our momentum takes off.

Laser-like focus means aligning your thinking habits, belief structures, feelings, and behaviors together with the mission. If you want financial independence, you need to align yourself with the goals of it, along with your heart, and wallet.

Avoid aiming in two directions at the same time and start focusing like a laser. If you want to take a trip to Panama, and be financially independent, you may have to rethink the strategy. Align your goals, and be focused like a laser, going in one direction.

Why is it necessary to focus? You may be wondering why maintaining a laser focus is necessary. Here are four essential benefits of maintaining a laser focus:

Achieve Greater Result

No one likes halfway performances. The consequence, which is only 99.9 percent, is a symbol of mediocrity. You can only achieve excellence if you understand your vision to the fullest. And that means having a laser beam. Great achievements are created by maintaining attention, and the results will be amplified.

Generate Faster Outcome

If you want to get results and fast (financial independence is not a fast journey), you'll need to avoid the temptation to purchase the shiny new corvette, for now anyway. Getting a laser-like concentration will help you always achieve results in a shorter amount of time.

Achieve Predicable Results

When you concentrate all your attention on one task, like a laser that generates a single light, you master the art of consistently producing quality results. Do you want to be average at several things, or a master at one thing? While results in financial markets are not predictable, as past performance is not indicative of future results, time in the markets, and with historical trends, the performance trends speak for themself. Of course, due diligence in the market, along with risk tolerance is to be evaluated.

Enjoy Peace of Mind

Lack of direction and concentration is always going to lead to uncertainty, but a laser-like focus eliminates clutter and distraction and gives you a clean sheet to work with, every day.

How can I maintain laser-like focus?

- Be clear about your view.

- Set up your game plan.

- Identify and concentrate on the most important activities.

When clarity is obtained, and the mission is clear, you can now define the tasks that are the most important. These are the tasks to prioritize.

Concentrate on what's important — thinking patterns, behaviors, and methods that deliver the quickest route, is the focus. Focus on things that will carry you forward, and remove tasks that withdraw your attention. Remember to say, "No."

The same strategy of getting financially fit, or making healthier food choices can be said of investing. The muscle of a laser-focus grows over time. Just as you won't wake up with a six pack after two weeks of training, you won't find a million dollars in your account after just a few months of investing. Delayed gratification with a laser focused growth mindset, in essence is the art of giving up short-term satisfaction, in order to gain a greater long-term reward.

How can we avoid failure on the journey toward financial independence?

As illogical as it may sound, failing to achieve our goals, can set the stage for our future successes, provided that we view these setbacks as lessons and not as signs of failures to come. We can learn from mistakes and perceived failures. Most failures are really learning opportunities. We really didn't fail, we learned what not to do.

If the goal is to achieve financial freedom by 50 years old (or sooner), and you have not achieved it, you may feel like you have failed. You may feel all sorts of mixed emotions, to include being sad, ashamed, downcast, discouraged or just down right distraught. We can also be paralyzed or convince ourselves that the struggle is not worth the reward. But resilience research shows that courage and persistence seem to be as predictive of success, and that those who succeed the most are the most determined. (Fleming & Ledogar, 2008).

If you believe you have failed, or have faced a setback or have run in to something that you could not control (stock market fluctuations, housing market changes etc.), take it an opportunity for your growth mindset to kick in. Things will happen on our journey to financial independence, interpret it as such, and adapt, and change as needed. Setbacks are actually progress; as if it occurs again (like the 2008 housing market collapse), you will be better suited next time a downturn in the market occurs. We may not be able to avoid "failure" but it's how we process it that matters.

Failure as Opportunity

The first thing to do after a failure is to become aware of it. Failure is a part of the process of success, and therefore inevitable. It should not discourage you and demoralize you. And even when a setback occurs, you have to do everything to regain your motivation and your relentlessness for the task. Each person must be prepared to be faced with bad luck, defeats, or obstacles. And this, despite the efforts made, it is important to take responsibility for the situation.

Don't blame anyone, and don't try to justify yourself by blaming others. You must be mature enough to be aware and take 100% responsibility for your perceived failure. This will allow you to get up better afterwards and regain the motivation to move forward. You decide what constitutes a true failure. Again, failure is not really failure as many define it, it's a learning experience.

We often think that failure is not obtaining the desired result by a certain time frame, or not achieving the predetermined and measured level of success by society. Perhaps you are concerned that you have not started a retirement account or 401(k) through your work yet and you feel it's too late to start. Maybe you are in your 40's and you have no savings and no emergency fund. Start today. We cannot go back in time. We have from this day forward, (own it) and make the changes necessary to begin.

We learn from our mistakes and we determine we will improve and move forward based on new information. It's about our mindset, and our inner character, which will carry us through challenges, and it will have the biggest impact on our future outcomes.

This idea of failure, does not consider the fact that one decides for oneself what constitutes a mistake or a misstep. We decide what is failure or what is a success. Failure is just one side of the coin. Can you flip the coin? What often appears to be short-term setback, can often be the single most important factor that creates the highway for momentum.

Next, we will discuss the impact of divorce on the plan of achieving financial independence. With today's estimates 50% of marriages are ending in divorce, it's a healthy component to discuss in the plan as divorce may have a major impact of financial matters with the pursuit to financial independence.

Starting Over After a Divorce

Divorce occurs in 50% of marriages and the impact of it, can alter the plans for financial independence (Marriage and Divorce, 2020). So now, what do you do if you are headed in this direction or already have completed the process? How does divorce impact the path to financial independence? Will I still be able to retire early?

Divorce will have an impact on financial independence and the pursuit along with our mindset. This may be a perceived setback or it may be the best thing that has happened with your finances. Maybe it is your wake-up call. As we have just discussed, our mindset is imperative to our success, and this process of divorce or separation can take its own unique toll. While it's a painful process for many, self-care, making wise decisions during the time and coming back with a firm foundation, will help to ease back into the pursuit of independence, financially speaking.

Perhaps you have recently divorced, and you find yourself alone. Divorce, when it occurs, is most always a painful process. Like any separation, divorce is one of the most stressful events in life. According to the Holmes Rahe Stress Inventory, divorce ranks number two on their scale (Holmes- Rahe Stress Inventory 2020). Separating from the person you love, with whom you thought you would spend the rest of your life, is quite difficult to say the least.

Overnight, your life changes and all your habits change. Things will be different going forward. Nothing will be the same again. Separation is a painful experience to go through. You are quite capable of facing this challenge. Reassess your financial goals and make the necessary steps to your budget when ready. There is no rush through in this process. Take your time and when ready move forward back on the journey toward the mission.

After you have come to terms with your separation, you must face the pain. From the first moments, you will be overwhelmed by a multitude of emotions: sadness, guilt, questioning, etc. Give yourself a time to pass the pain. Some psychologists advise writing down all the feelings generated by negative emotions, as it helps to break free. Once you have accepted feeling the negative emotions, you will have to mourn the relationship. The acceptance phase will take a long time, weeks, even months.

Rebuilding your life after the divorce will also force you to regain control over your emotions and to have confidence in yourself again. There are no miracle recipes, just everyday attitudes, and behaviors that you will have to adopt to get better. Surround yourself with supportive family and friends. To start a new life after divorce, is to start a new life, and to be a new person. Find your passions, interests, indulge in activities that make you happy, and that fill your life. Why not start an activity that you dreamed of doing and that you had to put off because of your relationship? Don't hesitate to embark on new projects.

Our mindset has the largest impact our future successes. Obtaining a growth mindset propels us forward, and our momentum is the fire that lights the path. Setbacks, perceived failures and relationship turnovers, can take us off the course for a time. Life wouldn't be so much fun without all the challenges, which will make us stronger, more fit financially (and perhaps otherwise), and will set us on a journey to achieve greater results, better than anticipated. We will go farther, faster and run at an outstanding pace, when we are laser focused, and are on a mission.

The journey to financial independence, with the ability to retire early, will not be met without challenges. It puts the hair on our chest. We are more adaptable, and see the big picture in front of our face. Financial independence brings us the freedom to spend our time, how we want, with who we want, and it is a token to create the future we wish to have.

Next, we will discuss investing in the stock market along with precious metal alternatives as investment vehicles, plus is cryptocurrency a wise choice?

Chapter Three

Stock Market and Investing

"If you get to my age in life and nobody thinks well of you, I don't care how big your bank account is, your life is a disaster." Warren Buffett

I nvesting in the stock market is one of the financial tools to increase wealth, and can lead to financial independence. This investment tool allows, among other things, to receive income and to profit from capital gains. An investor can receive dividends, which represent a part of the company's profits, if buying shares. One can also receive bond coupons, which represent a payment of interest, the bonds being loans made by investors to issuers. In addition, an investor, derives profits if he sells a security at a higher price than he bought it, because of the evolution of the price of the security on the market. The basic rules of investing include:

1. Invest the savings you don't need. Given the risk incurred, individuals should invest in the stock market (index funds) a fraction of savings to which they can do without. The stock market has risks and loss can occur. Choose to invest wisely with careful diligence on the options chosen.

2. Research the different stocks before choosing to invest.

It is important to be educated on the risk level of each stock, expense ratio, historical trends (which is no indication of future performance), financial status of companies, before investing. Companies are required to communicate their financial information to the public on a regular basis which can be quarterly, etc.

3. Have an investment strategy. Before investing, come up with a plan. Determine what profit, target and maximum floor, for your risk tolerance.

4. Diversify your portfolio. Many choose a mix of stocks, bonds, index funds, and mutual funds, and exchange traded funds, etc. Diversification helps to offset the risk associated with the portfolio. You can choose to invest heavier in stocks for example, and less and in bonds and then as you are nearing retirement, you may wish to reallocate to have a greater percentage into bonds.

5. Log into your account often – but not too often. The stock market can have wide swings from time to time, but there is a saying, time in the market beats timing the market. While it is not possible to time the market, it is important to check your investments to track movement in the markets and to keep an eye on it (Online, *Stock Market Investment: 10 things you must know before investing in stock markets* 2018).

Risks and Precautions

Risk is associated with all forms of investments. It is advisable to be well informed and know how financial products work, before investing in the stock market. Usually, an investment with a high return potential carries greater risk. Some investments can result in a total loss of invested capital, or even, for the riskiest investments, a loss greater than invested capital.

How to Invest in a 401(k)

1. Contact your Employer

Many employers have an auto-enrollment feature in their 401(k) plan, which comes to a surprise to some employees. An employee may opt out, or change their deferral rate, according to the 401 (k) plan provider.

If there is auto-enrollment, a predetermined percentage of your pretax paycheck, will be contributed to your 401(k). The default percentage rate depends on the company's plan specifics, but can range up to 5 percent per pay period.

To find out if you're enrolled in your company 401(k), check your pay stub or contact your human resources team, or review your offer letter and terms discussed at time of hire. If you are not enrolled in your company's 401 (k), enroll. Contact your HR representative or Benefits Team member to enroll in your 401 (k) plan. They can provide guidance on the enrollment process and plan specifics.

2. See if Your Employer Offers a Company Match

Ask your HR team or representative for information on employer contribution match and exactly how it is calculated and the timing.

3. Take Note of Your Employer's Vesting Schedule

Any contributions you make to a 401(k) are yours to keep, although you won't be able to access the money before age 59 and 1/2 without incurring a penalty (usually 10% penalty if withdrawn prior to) and/or paying income tax.

Contributions your employer makes to your 401(k), including matches, may not be yours right away, this is due to the company's specific vesting schedule. Your 401(k) plan's vesting schedule will outline when your employer's contributions will be yours. Some company contributions may not be available for 4 years for example with 25 percent available incrementally each year.

Contact your human resources team to understand your company's vesting schedule. If you leave the company before being fully vested, you'll lose a portion, or all of your employer's contribution that hasn't already been vested.

4. Select a Deferral Percentage

Many people are undecided when it comes to how much to contribute toward their 401(k), but anything is better than nothing. When it comes to the Financial Independence, Retire Early mindset, it's an absolute must to max out 401(k) contributions annually. If you cannot max out your 401 (k) contributions annually, make the steps to increase your percentage. Start off with your current contribution and the following month, increase your percentage by 1% next month and so on. Keep going and keep contributing until you have maxed out your contribution limit for the year.

In 2020 and for 2021, the IRS allows employees to contribute $19,500 to a 401(k), plus the IRS allows for a catch-up amount of $6,500. if over age 50 (Kagan, 2020). To max out your 401(k) this year, you'd need to contribute about $812 every paycheck (assuming 24 bi-monthly paychecks over the course of the calendar year). Please check the IRS guidelines as changes do occur from time to time.

5. Select a Beneficiary

Choose a beneficiary — this is the person or family member who would inherit your 401(k) in the event of your death. A beneficiary can be changed at any time.

6. Browse Investment Options and Review Fee Schedule

Investments in a 401(k) are selected by the employer. There are two general types of fees you will see in your account:

- Fee for account management charged directly by the 401(k)-plan provider

- Fee charged by the mutual funds and Exchange Traded Funds (ETFs) in your 401(k) account (expense ratio), the lower the expense ratio the better, however do research to see what funds are best to invest in

(Many on the F.I.R.E. path choose to invest in VTSAX, but not all 401(k) providers through employee sponsored custodians offer it. There are other options which have similar performance, such as the S&P index fund. I have heard many employees reaching out to their employer to have VTSAX offered in their 401 (k) plans. Talk to your fellow employees, and if it's not offered, see if they can make changes with the plan to make it available.)

In your 401(k), the account management fee is unavoidable. If your provider is charging a management fee above 1% of your account assets, you may consider directing your savings elsewhere, such as an IRA with lower fees. However, it could be worth contributing if your employer offers a match, that is higher than the provider's management fee. These are all things to keep in mind to find the best investment vehicles to park your hard-earned money.

Most mutual funds charge a management fee, as well. On each investment fund, listed as expense ratio, or the fee rate as a percent of assets. Choose funds with an expense ratio below 1%, otherwise the fees could start eating into your returns.

7. Select Investments

Apart from fees, there are two important factors to consider when choosing specific investment vehicles: time and risk tolerance. It's important to ascertain how much time (years) you will be invested in the market vs the level of risk in your holdings.

8. Select Contributions Threshold per Investment

As you choose your specific investment vehicles, you'll decide how much of your contributions will go toward each investment, usually expressed as a percentage. If you only choose one fund, 100% of your money will be invested in that fund. If you create a portfolio with three different funds, you can decide what percentage of your contributions will go toward each fund.

9. Observe the Market and Earnings Periodically

You can change your contribution rate and manage your investments by logging on to your account, through your plan provider's website (e.g., Vanguard, Fidelity, etc.). Most experts suggest increasing your 401(k)-contribution rate at least once a year, or each time you get a raise (Loudenback, 2019).

Now that we have discussed investing in 401(k), we will look at other investment vehicles.

Individual Retirement Accounts

After maxing out your 401(k) for the calendar year, max out your Roth Individual Retirement Account (Roth IRA). The max contribution for 2020 is $6,000 per person. A spouse may also be able to contribute toward their spouse's IRA. Please check the contribution limits, as these do change from time to time, and consult your tax professional on income restrictions.

There are two types of Individual Retirement Accounts, or IRA's. There is a traditional IRA and a Roth IRA. A Roth IRA is an after-tax investment vehicle, whereas a Traditional IRA allows for pre-tax funds. Having a Roth IRA provides for an additional investment vehicle outside your 401 (k) plan.

Taxable Brokerage Accounts

After your 401(k) and IRA's has been fully funded, consider opening a taxable brokerage account. With a taxable brokerage account, you can contribute additional funds in the stock market. On the same token, please also be sure to have an emergency fund in place, typically 3-6 months of monthly savings, in case your plan goes awry, or due to loss of income, or health emergency (Loudenback, 2019).

Roth Conversion Ladder

When you are planning to retire early and need to be able to live off the funds in your investment, a Roth Ladder, or a Roth Conversion is an option to explore. When you have funds in your company-sponsored retirement plan, or 401 (k), the money you contribute (with an additional employer match) is on a pre-tax basis. You will not have to pay taxes on it until age 59 ½. If you take fund out of your 401(k), there may be a 10% penalty on your investments. Due to the recent global situation, there have been some updates for withdrawals on your 401 (k), be sure to familiarize yourself with the recent changes.

If your goal is to retire before age 59 ½ you may not be able to access the funds in your 401 (k) until you have reached this age requirement. This means you won't have access to touch your money until decades after you intend to retire if you choose to retire in your 30's for example. For many this is too long to wait, and there another option, which is the Roth conversion.

A Roth conversion moves funds from a 401(k) to a Traditional IRA to a Roth IRA, without any penalties. This option works by converting funds from a 401(k) to a Traditional IRA to a Roth and withdrawing the principal portion after five years. The best part of this ladder is you will be able to withdraw funds from your 401(k) and Roth IRA earlier than 59 1/2 — allowing you to use your money earlier and retire as soon as possible (Sethi, 2020). If you plan to do a Roth conversion, its best to speak to your CPA, or tax accountant, as they can provide further details and even provide the best timing, to move funds based on your taxable income and investments for the year.

VTSAX – The Vanguard Group

The Vanguard's Total Stock Market Index (VTSAX) is a popular mutual fund for many in the F.I.R.E. community and with a good cause. It has been reported that VTSAX is the largest mutual fund in the world. It is one of the most well-run and has provided investors with simple, low-cost diversification to the entire U.S. stock market. (Physician, 2019).

Historically, VTSAX has performed with an annual rate of return of 9.74%, since its inception in 1992 (at the time of this writing). VTSAX includes small, mid and large cap stocks, which provides investors a broad level aspect of the market, coupled with low expense ratios.

VTSAX currently offers approximately 3590 individual stocks, with a weighted average, which means with the larger the fund, the greater of a weight it carries toward the total percentage of the investment. Currently, VTSAX consists of some of the largest companies to include Apple, Microsoft Corp., Amazon and Facebook, and has a low expense ratio of 0.04% (Uppaluri, 2020).

Many proponents in the F.I.R.E., community invest in VTSAX solely or a high percentage of assets, but there are some good alternatives with other low-cost brokerage firms, such as Fidelity

Investments and Charles Schwab. Fidelity recently introduced zero expense ratios on several investments: FNILX (Fidelity Zero Large Cap Index Fund); FZILX (Fidelity Zero International Index); FZIPX (Fidelity Zero Extended Market Index); and FZROX (Fidelity Zero Total Market Index). These may be wise choices for investors, due to the expense ratio and performance. FZROX is closely assimilated to VTSAX. Charles Schwab has SWTSX (Schwab Total Stock Market Index Fund), or SWPPX which is the Schwab version of the Schwab 500 S&P Index Fund.

What about investing in precious metals, such a gold and silver?

Invest in Gold/Silver

We often hear about investing in precious metals such as gold and silver. Are you wondering whether it's better to invest in gold or silver? Or neither, or both?

If you have little cash on hand, you will be more likely to invest in silver, which is approximately 76 times cheaper than an ounce of gold (for the same weight). At the time of this writing, 1 oz. of gold comes in at approx. $1,867 while silver rings the bell at $2 4.51 an oz. (Gold Price, 2020). Although gold is more costly than silver, it has a serious advantage: it offers a better concentration of values. In other words, with a $1,000 investment in gold, it takes up much less space than the same value invested in silver.

When you choose to invest in gold or silver, or other precious metals for example copper, you also have to think about storage. If you decide to keep your precious metals at home, you will have anticipate acquiring a sufficiently large safe to hold the items. You may also have the possibility of storing precious metals with custodians around the country. The storage costs will be higher for silver than for gold, merely due to volume. Review the storage fees if you decide to have them stored in an off-site location.

While gold is a relatively safe investment, silver is much less so. Although silver is used much more than gold, which seems to be a great sign for investors, the risks of loss are significant. Indeed, it is possible to win, but also to lose enormously, by investing in precious metals.

Converting dollars into silver or physical gold may seem wise for investors who have little cash. Silver displays an attractive and reasonable cost and as for gold, it is possible to buy it in small quantities, such as in grams. Be careful, however, not to allocate your entire portfolio to precious metals, and even less with silver. Silver is more volatile than gold, and is more expensive to store.

Invest in Cryptocurrency

Investing in cryptocurrency is a high-risk activity for your finances: there is no certainty about the gains made by any particular investment, and many buyers lose their stake. Historically the first virtual currency created in 2008, in response to the economic crisis that hit the world, bitcoin (BTC) remains the safest value for investing.

On the heels of bitcoin is Ethereum (ETH), pioneer of Decentralized Finance (DeFi), which actually has more users on its blockchain than the king of bitcoin! Who's next? The nano (NANO), and its many possible transactions per second, is attracting more and more people, but the hack it suffered in 2018, has seriously shaken its value. Tezos (XTZ), which relies on the security and rigor of its program to offer investors, has attractive returns. Or, take a look at the Basic Attention Token (BAT) which exceeded 10 million active users at the end of 2019 (Cointelegraph, 2020).

It is very important to come back to one of the essential points of investing in cryptocurrency: risk appetite. Crypto assets such as bitcoin, the Basic Attention Token or the Nexo all involve risk of loss. So, be prepared to lose your entire stake in the worst case!

It is strongly recommended to learn in detail about the functioning of the financial markets of the cryptocurrency, on the related decentralized applications or on each of the crypto assets that you wish to acquire. Entering an online community (typically on Reddit or Slack) also allows you to interact with other users and learn more about the pros and cons of investing in cryptocurrency.

If you are familiar with how the Stock Exchange works, there will be no secrets for you here. The regular buying and selling of crypto assets are reserved for investors who know the system and the financial markets inside out. The goal? Over a short period of time, buy an asset when its value is at the bottom of a curve (which is falling) and sell it when its value rises.

An Unforeseen Factor: The New Global Situation

Financial Independence means different things to different people, whether free-falling at the end of the bungee cord, choosing to retire early and explore the world, or having the means to support oneself without relying on others. Yet, the current global situation of 2020, has curbed many of the liberties that we have taken for granted. Although the situation is continuing to progress, many restrictions are in place. For many, the sense of financial independence has been stripped away, whether because of abrupt work losses or wage cuts, or because of the grim economic environment.

It is in this already fragile economic context that the pandemic came to be grafted, the spread of the coronavirus continues to hamper economic activity internationally. China was the first to see its economy slow down, with major repercussions on all economic activity globally. Many companies in the world are dependent on China, their activity is directly impacted, and the global economic outlook is being revised to adjust. Italy was then confined, then, little by little, all the countries of the world. The economic repercussions are, and will be very serious, and the specter of a global recession is now clearly a reality.

The fall in stock prices in March 2020, and the extreme volatility that we are seeing today in the markets reflect this very uncertain economic situation. Economic uncertainty is greatly amplified by the health crisis in itself, and the many legitimate concerns it gives rise to. It is also reinforced by the plunge in oil prices; the latter having made the markets aware of the seriousness of the looming economic situation.

If the coronavirus certainly first impacted the real sphere, with the slowdown in global economic activity, and then affected the financial markets, the fact remains that the financial crisis was latent. The pandemic has accelerated its outbreak. Moreover, a boomerang effect is to be expected, with the risk of entering a "vicious circle." The very strong economic slowdown we are witnessing is indeed pushing many investors to sell their shares. By doing so, they fuel and deepen the downside in the markets, again spilling over to the real economy by further weakening firms. These phenomena, well known in finance, refer to what economists call self-fulfilling prophecies.

For those in the 30's and 40's, the economic consequences of the pandemic have been more serious. With many losing their jobs, or having to reevaluate their plan. Bankruptcies, and consequently the associated massive job losses, will then be inevitable with a chain of defaults capable of producing a systemic risk. While it is obviously far too early to know what the duration and extent of the expected recession will be, all means must be implemented to revive growth and business investment, both on the part of the monetary authorities and at the level of government measures.

The economic recession is inevitable and the question of the severity of the financial crisis is obviously linked to the risk of default on corporate debt. The major crisis will be even more disastrous if banks suspend their credit to businesses, and if they stop interbank lending. This is a time when more people are seeing the benefits of being financially independent. If things take a turn for the worse, or hopefully better, they are in a strong financial position to overcome the market's volatility.

Next, real estate investing has always been a hot topic in the F.I.R.E. community. We will discuss ways to get involved in real estate along with the famous BRRRR approach.

Chapter Four

Real Estate Investing- BRRRR Style

"The secret to success in life is that a man is ready to seize the opportunity that presents itself."
Benjamin Disraeli

I nvesting in real estate is one of the few assets that can be acquired through the use of credit or a mortgage. When looking to invest in property it's optimal to review several layers of risk and to determine the length of time you wish to hold the asset.

Both long-term real estate investing and short-term have pros and cons. When you buy investment property you must determine your exit strategy, and when you wish to sell it. In the vast majority of situations, investing in rentals would be worthwhile over the long term, that is, for several years.

There are many ways to make money with real estate investing: Either by the valuation of the investment, which is likely to increase (the objective is then to generate a capital gain on resale), or by income from property that is earned by rents after deduction of taxes and charges.

Rental properties should be reviewed in your local area as well as out of state. You need to take into account the local rental market, the developments in the area (is it progressing well? Is it going to be more appealing in a few years, is there a new shopping mall going in?). Also, it's imperative to measure its rental profitability. This will allow you to research, to compare and contrast hot markets, verses investment properties in conservative areas across the country. You will see that depending on the city you want to buy and rent your home, the average return would not be the same. Strong differences will occur from one region to another.

As you begin to explore rental opportunities, it is not about investing in the first apartment for sale that you will see, and renting it to make a profit and collect your first dollar. The real estate market is not always profitable: high prices, low returns, taxes and often low tenant/landlord rights in the face of bad tenants, etc. It is important to make a very accurate selection of the property. This is the first golden rule in a successful real estate investment, especially in a context of historical low interest rates, where housing prices are high in relation to income and rents.

One of the best rules of thumb to evaluate whether an investment property is a solid purchase, is the use the one percent rule. The one percent rule is a guideline which estimates the future rental income vs. the purchase price of the property. The rule states the rental income derived from the property, should be equal to or greater than the one percent, of the purchase price. For example, if you purchase a property for $140,000 and can rent it for $1,400 this would satisfy this 1 percent rule. This of course will not include separate housing expenses that are part of the process of owning real estate such as closing costs, general maintenance, property insurance and taxes and down payment (Team, 2020). This rule; however, should not be the only measure to judge whether an investment property will be suitable. A full evaluation of the market, neighborhood, area attractions, plus your goal of property ownership, to include your short- and long-term goals should be considered.

When you have taken the first step and have located a property to buy, you have to rent it out. For that, it is necessary to define a rent. Attractive enough to find a tenant quickly and easily, but as high as possible to obtain the best profitability. It's all about the right balance between these two needs. You will then have to prepare a rental agreement, and get set up with the administrative side of the business and be ready to be a landlord. Finally, you will need to find a tenant. There are many means of prospecting for this. You will be able to choose your tenant and quickly set up the lease in order to start collecting rent without having rental vacancy.

What is the BRRRR Approach to Investing in Real Estate?

If you are interested in real estate or plan to start a real estate investment company, you will eventually learn about BRRRR or Buy, Rehabilitate, Rent, Refinance and Repeat. This method of investing in rental properties has increased in popularity over the last decade and focuses on finding distressed properties to purchase, rehabilitate, rent, refinance, and then to repeat the process on another property.

The BRRRR method of investing in real estate has proven to be a great way to create cash flow, and financial freedom through rental income, but it's not the best fit for everybody.

What is the Buy, Rehabilitate, Rent, Refinance, Repeat (BRRRR) Real Estate Strategy?

The BRRRR strategy for investing in real estate is to purchase, rehabilitate, rent, refinance and repeat. This investment strategy is suitable for investors who want to develop a broad portfolio of rental properties rapidly and operates in the following manner:

Buy: acquisition of undervalued or undervalued assets with alternative funding, such as hard money lending.

Rehab: Make value-added changes to the property to get it ready for sale.

Rent: Rent the property to industry expectations.

Refinance: Use cash-out refinancing to pay off your initial hard money loan.

Repeat: Use the profit left over from cash-out refinancing as a fresh down payment on your next investment house.

Advantages of BRRRR

BRRRR Investing helps you to expand an investment portfolio without having to expend huge amounts of cash for a long period of time. Traditionally, if you were to buy five rental properties, you would need a down payment for each of the five properties. With this approach, you can still expand a portfolio of five rental properties, but you're dispensing much less cash than with the conventional investment process.

Because this strategy involves cash-out refinancing, after the property has been renovated and leased, you can withdraw your capital to reinvest in another property, with the advantage of a long-term mortgage, that has little or none of your money invested in it. In addition, if you own rental land, you may now benefit from a variety of tax deductions.

If done correctly, the BRRRR approach, has the ability to increase your net worth, produce passive income through rental income, and eventually create financial independence by allowing you to own rental property in a unique and continuous manner.

No form of investing is foolproof. BRRRR Real Estate Investments do come with disadvantages, perhaps the biggest of which is that your investment depends on future value. If the property value during the refinancing process is lower than expected, you may not be able to refinance the maximum sum you want.

Another possible risk is that renovations will take longer than expected. If you've ever rehabilitated your house, you know it's pretty normal to have extra costs due to unforeseen but required repairs or extended timelines.

If you borrow money from a hard money lender, you're paying high fees and high interest rates than a typical conventional loan. The longer your hard money loan is intact, the less money you make. Some hard money loans have unfavorable terms such as a balloon payment after a certain number of months. Moving in and out of the transaction as soon as possible is a key component of the success of this investment process.

If you're interested in starting to develop a rental portfolio using the BRRRR investment strategy, here's how to get started.

Buy

The first move you need to do take, is find a suitable investment property to purchase. For this approach to be practical, you need to find a property that is undervalued or that can be dramatically increased with renovations. Buy at a discount — a steep discount. There are a lot of ways to purchase properties outside the market, or within the Multiple Listing Services (MLS).

It's suggested that you stick to the importance of the after-repair value (ARV) formula used when flipping homes, to ensure that the property has plenty of space for additional capital after repair. Perform a detailed review of the rental to ensure that the property makes sense as a long-term rental. The BRRRR model is for rental assets, so the ARV formula alone is not the only measure to determine if a property is suitable to purchase.

When you find the right investment opportunity, you're going to need to buy it. This means obtaining support. As the property needs to be restored, it may be impossible to qualify for a conventional mortgage. Most investors use private equity, or hard-money loans, to fund their BRRRR investments. This is a more costly choice for funding, but it has fewer underwriting requirements than a bank or a conventional lender.

A hard money loan would also require the cost of rehabilitation. It's better to save about 20% of the overall loan for a down payment, and don't forget the budget for closing costs. If you find a lot, maybe you don't need to put too much down, but it's a good goal to get started. There are several online calculators to help determine if a property is suitable for the BRRRR approach of investing.

Rehab

Next move is to rehab the house. Try to complete the recovery as soon as possible. This keeps costs down and helps you to start making cash out of the property sooner. Note that this property is owned for rental income and does not require the bells and whistles of a full-blown rehab house. Make your home clean, beautiful, and livable but you may not need to install granite countertops, for example.

Rent

After the renovation has been completed, you can rent the house. It's not always easy to be a landlord. Before agreeing to become a landlord, do your due diligence on what owning the rental property means, and how to be a good landlord. Please check with city and county ordinances along with any applicable state guidelines. Be sure you have a lease agreement.

Refinance

After the property is secured with the tenant, and you have several months of rental history, you can start the refinancing process. Refinancing can be the most difficult aspect of the BRRRR system, as certain lenders may have particular criteria for the refinancing phase.

Repeat

Ideally, the investment in BRRRR will go as expected and you will have bought, rehabilitated, leased and refinanced the property, without a hitch. If that is so, then the time has come to roll your initial investment into a new investment property. If you've done a very nice job, you should have extra money left over that can go into your wallet, or be reinvested in your real estate investment business.

Is the BRRRR method profitable?

How much money you make when using BRRRR strategy depends on how successful you are at getting the right properties to purchase at the right price. As with every investment plan, returns, income, and expenses can differ significantly; however, the better you are at following quality leads, assessing investment and maintaining and rehabilitating assets, the better the performance would be.

There are a variety of moving parts of this investment plan, and a lot of ways that things could go wrong. It is necessary that you practice due diligence on the specific investment strategies used by the BRRRR investment method before you attempt to buy a property using the BRRRR method.

While the BRRRR method has many success stores, the recent global events have some rethinking the strategy while others have gone full force, picking up multiple properties during this time. There are many who are waiting for a downturn in property values, and are stacking up the cash now, to position themselves to purchase in the future.

While considering the BRRRR approach its best to review city/state ordinances for how rental income and the landlord/tenant relationship has been impacted and will continue to progress, which leads us to the next topic.

The BRRRR style of investing with real estate is one of the great ways to achieve financial independence. By increasing viable and passive income streams, you are on your way of impacting your financial future and taking another step toward retiring early and creating your future one simple step at a time. We are going to take a look at some practical changes we can do today to get started toward financial independence.

Chapter Five

23 Practical Changes

"FOCUS - Take a course until you pass." Robert
Kiyosaki

T he pathway to financial independence, with the ability to retire early, is made with a series of simple, small steps. It is not rocket science, and it is not necessarily a new concept. The basic concept is to save more (abundantly more), than what is spent every month, and to invest it. It's to have a budget and a plan, with the long-term favorable goal of being free from either the 9-5 daily grind, or free to work for yourself, create a business or to take a hiatus and travel. Your assets along with passive income sources will allow you to have the flexibility and freedom your life demands. The choice in how you spend your time in retirement is completely up to you.

Financial independence breeds choice and opportunity. We are going to breakdown several practical steps to obtain financial independence so you can retire early.

Save Regularly and Invest Abundantly

To be financially free, it is essential to save regularly, regardless of the level of your monthly income. So instead of indulging in unnecessary expenses, save money on a regular basis, and save big. The more saved, the sooner your savings can grow allowing for compound interest to do its magic. Many in the F.I.R.E.

community save upward of 70 percent of their income each month (Adcock, 2020).

Abundant saving is to build a fantastic future. The greater the percentage of savings, the faster the mission is accomplished. Like all things in life, the culture of saving is learned over time. It's okay to not start off with saving 70 percent of your income on day 1. Can you save 10 percent? 20 percent? Think of the day when you will save 50 percent. Take the conscious effort to lay out a savings plan for today with incremental increases. If you receive a bonus from work can you invest it? Make the effort to integrate it into your life until saving becomes a habit.

Set a goal, see how fast you can save and invest an additional $10,000. Will it take 3 months? 6 months? Can you live without Netflix for a time? Do you really need that much from Costco? I used to shop at Costco. When I would go, I remember telling myself that I only needed two things. When I left the store, I had over $200 of stuff that I claimed that I needed. I don't know about you, but it's like something is sucking me in to buy more when I go to Costco. Do you really need to eat steak once a week? Sometimes it's the little things that we can cut out for a while, that will have a huge impact on the goal.

The Magic of Compound Interest

One of the main ways our investments grow in the stock market is through compound interest. Compound interest is the secret to financial independence. The longer your investments are in the market, and the longer they have to grow, the greater your results will be. Again, I am not a financial advisor, but let's talk a little bit on how compound interest works.

Say, for example, you have $20,000 invested in VTSAX with a 10% rate of return, which compounds annually, without contributions other than the initial investment. I am going to use simple math for the sake of illustration. At the end of year one, you will have $22,000 ($20,000 x .10 = $2,000, and $20,000

+ $2,000 = $22,000) invested in the market. The $20,000 is the initial investment and the $2,000 is the interest earned. When year 2 occurs, you will now have $22,000 as your starting point. Assuming the same rate of return, 10%, you will now have $24,200, due to the impact of compound interest. After 10 years, the sum you will have will be $51,874.85. This is the magic of compound interest.

Now, let's add a twist. Let's take the same initial investment of $20,000 and incrementally add $1,000 to it each month, all other factors the same, same rate of return, and compounded annually. Year 1, your initial investment of $20,000 is now $34,000. Year 2, $49,400, and after 10 years, an outstanding $243,123.94.

Let's do another scenario. Say your investment today is $100,000 the stock market, with all other factors the same; how soon will it take you to retire, if your magic number is $1M? If you do not contribute any additional capital, it will take 25 years to reach $1,083.470.59. The more funds contributed, the sooner you will be financially free. If you invest $1,000 a month into your investment portfolio, you will be able to retire in 18 years having $1,103,181.81. If you want to retire earlier, and contribute $2,000 a month, you can retire in 14 years. Let's say, you embrace frugality, and you invest heavily with $5,000 a month; you will have $1,050,563.38 in 9 years (*Compound Interest Calculator* 2020).

Embrace Frugal Mindset

Now, that you see how much your money can grow over time, and with incremental contributions in your investment portfolio, you may be thinking, how you can add even more to your investments. This is where frugality comes into play and to the brave, extreme frugality.

Stephan Graham, real estate agent and investor, one who embraces the BRRRR approach to real estate investing, became a millionaire by the time he was 26. Currently he has 2.59 million subscribers on his YouTube channel discussing all things financially related – real estate investing, stock market updates and the like. Do you think he is in line at the Starbucks drive-thru every day getting his Venti Mocha Flat White Coffee? He has a video on how he became a millionaire, is not an advocate for Starbucks, but brews his $.20 coffee, you guessed it, at home (Graham, 2018). Has he embraced frugality? You better believe it.

Frugality is not just a notion to see how much less we can live on per say, but it's driven by pure motivation to have other things that are deemed more important in life. Sure, there are many who choose to live frugality for environmental reasons, or even other reasons. For many in the F.I.R.E. community, they will say, "No" to many things, live in a smaller house, shop for essentials only when needed, and take a hard stance to reduce cost. They take on the mindset of frugality, with the hope of getting out of the rat race, starting their business, traveling and being financially independent. By choosing to embrace frugality, one can be on the pathway to financial freedom and independence sooner, than the standard pathway many choose to follow, which is to retire by age 65. Do you want to wait until you are 65 to retire?

Let's say you visit Starbucks 3 times a month and spend $25, maybe you even pick up a coffee for a friend when you are there. Let's run the scenario with $100,000 starting point in your VT-SAX. Instead of visiting Starbucks and spending $25 a month, you invest it in VTSAX over the next 5 years. How much will your initial investment be after 5 years? Your initial $100,000 has grown (with a 10% rate of return), with compounding interest to be $162,882.53. After 10 years? If you keep investing the same $25 a month, after 10 years, you will have $264,155.47. The steady growth occurs through your contributions, as well as compounded interest, coupled with the rate of return, and time spent in the market. The earlier you can increase your investments, the longer it has time to grow.

Be Disciplined in Managing the Budget

To achieve financial independence, it's important to set a monthly budget and manage it well. Cutting back on household spending doesn't necessarily mean you have to cut back on your needs; figure out what's really needed and what isn't. The best idea is to cut back on recurring and non-temporary expenses, so your savings add up over time.

Break out the spreadsheet or use an online tool to evaluate monthly expenditures. Plan ahead for every penny spent and saved. Include investments in the budget. Make it fun. Sit down with your spouse every week or month and review the budget over a glass of wine.

Evaluate the previous month to note victories and improvements. Get creative and find ways to remove a line item on the budget and celebrate once occurred. Maybe it's time to put monthly subscriptions on hold for a season. Is amazon prime really a necessity? Be sure to include expenses that may not be paid out monthly such as taxes or insurance. Find ways to increase savings at every opportunity. Finding quick and painless ways to put money aside, without giving up essentials, and without feeling that you are sacrificing too much in your usual way of life is, one of the biggest challenges in personal finance.

Every month, as you shop, use your provisions wisely. Adjust your expenses with the means you currently have, and do not spend more than you make. Avoid relying on your next salary to incur debt. Plan for large purchases ahead of time. Think of when you will purchase your next vehicle and include it in the budget.

If you have saved $29, transfer this amount into your savings account (or stock portfolio) immediately, or apply it to any outstanding debt. Financial independence calls for serious, thorough budgeting to accomplish this task. You can't willy-nilly your way into financial independence. To have a plan and a budget is absolutely essential. You have to be able to see where your money goes every month vs. the income. Take the necessary steps to cut back for a time, and have intense focus on the mission. Your future self will thank you and you will look back and be stunned and amazed at how much you have accomplished.

Determination and Patience

Determination is a very useful skillset if, for a season, it allows you to deprive yourself of certain leisure activities to prioritize good financial habits. So, set achievable goals for yourself and do everything in your power to achieve and exceed them as soon as possible. Determination can make you wealthy (not alone), but it is helpful as it also corresponds with patience.

Financial freedom does not occur overnight. It is part of a gradual process that requires determination and patience. If results are slow in coming, carry the growth mindset forward to keep track of your goals. Keep at it. It's okay to have setbacks but keep going. It's the determination in keeping with the long-term goal, over the long haul. Keep going. Small changes turn into large sums after years with compounded interest. This mindset will help to overcome the hurdles faced along the way, and there will be many.

Persistence and Perseverance

Succeeding on the journey to financial independence, is not a one-way street or a straight line. It is a winding path with valleys and descents (think stock market). Market conditions change, property values shift, but with persistence over the long haul, you will eventually reach the objective. Difficulties and challenges will come. These challenges may get us off track and cause a setback, but we can learn through them, and pick back up where we left off. Keep going. Get back on track with your budget and savings goals and sprinkle on some massive perseverance.

Take Immediate Action

The strategies in this list up to this point and going forward are all going to require one thing. Action.

You can read this book every day, but it will not get you one step closer to your goal without implementing action. Taking action toward the goal of financial independence so you can retire early, is essential. You will not create wealth without taking action. You can read every book and blog article on the subject, until you are blue in the face, but again, it will not get you closer to the goal. Implement these steps today. Create the future you want. It will take time for wealth to build and grow and the journey will be worth it. Take action now.

Use Coupons and Discount Codes

Discount codes and coupons are helpful to save money. If you are planning to make an online purchase, there are many retailers that offer codes. Search the web for these codes, or wait until the item goes on sale. Timing large purchases, or even smaller purchases, will help to cut off expenses here and there.

Refrain from making an impulse purchase. Impulse purchases are typically not in the budget, and are an extra expense. At the checkout line there are many enticing last minute items we can easily justify to add to our cart, this is where self-control comes in, and also the determination, we spoke about earlier comes into play.

Think of how proud you will be when you have said, "No" to a purchase? Your willpower will start to grow into a strong muscle and it will eventually be easier to turn down those last-minute items, we claim we need.

Shop Discount Retailers

Discount retails such as Aldi or even the dollar store, can be used for many purchases. Many times, you can pick up a few items at these stores to save a bundle. If you prefer to shop at a regular grocery store consider the off-brand items, or the items on the lower shelves that are easily missed. Many times, their products are very similar as the brand-name items, but the packaging is different, without all the pretty colors. They are plain and ordinary, and you know what, they cost less. Your wallet will thank you.

There are some retailers that offer savings on certain days of the week. We have a grocery store chain in our area that offers double savings on Wednesday. Search out the shopping retailers in your area to see if they offer savings on certain days of the week.

If you are buying clothes, try to shop out of season or at the very end of the season. Many times, there will be huge sales as department stores are trying to make room for new seasonal items.

Alternative Locations to Purchase

Yard sales, Facebook marketplace, eBay are all good locations to find a great deal. Be open to new places to get an item for less. You may need to dig through online retailers or it may call for negotiating skills to get a lower price than listed at a yard sale, but that is also a handy new skill to pick up. At yard sales, may people just want to get rid of an item, and they anticipate having to lower the price a bit.

In fact, have your own yard sale, this is a great way to get rid of unused household items, and make a profit. You will also clear up space inside your home and reduce some clutter.

Have Fun for Less

Focusing on the mission of financial independence, so we can retire as early as possible doesn't mean we can't have fun. Fun is the spark of life, and without it, life can become dreary, boring and we can get complacent. Make fun a part of your life. Find new things that are enjoyable, for instance, many people that are in the F.I.R.E. community find it a game to see how much they can save, and they become financial nerds. This is fun for many, but not everyone.

When you have reached a goal, celebrate and celebrate in new way, and reward yourself favorably. Make the reward worth all the hard work you have put in. One couple I know made it a goal that whenever they hit a milestone, they would plan a trip. They loved to travel and made it part of their F.I.R.E. journey. They were not willing to cut travel out of their life. If you are passionate about seeing new parts of the county and want to explore, then do it.

On the same token, there are many fun activities that do not cost much or anything. When was the last time you took a leisurely walk in the park, or hiked a trail? When was the last time you went to a matinee? If you google "free activities in your local city/state" you will come up a whole host of fun things to do. Fun does not always need to cost money.

Reduce Monthly Expenses

Since the global event has been transpiring, many people are taking advantage of lower car and homeowner insurance rates. It's absolutely worth to call your current provider(s) to see if they can lower your current rate. Sometimes you can also raise your deductible which can help to reduce the overall cost. Too, since many are driving less, your car insurance policy may have an option if your vehicle is mostly parked in the garage, with a low mileage option. Call your providers today, and also shop around, to see how much you can save.

If you bundle your homeowners and car insurance together, also check to see what your policies would look like as separate. To my amazement, I was able to pay less for my policies by not bundling.

Next, contact your cell phone provider. I was with the same cell phone provider for the past 4 years. I decided to shop my current plan provider (after reviewing discount cell phone plan providers) and to my surprise, due to the recent global pandemic, my current cell phone provider created a new plan which allowed me to save over $50 a month. I switched to a prepaid plan and was able to keep my phone number; this is a savings of $600 a year.

Another option is to call your local internet provider. When you call, ask them to review your account for the past 30 days to check for internet outages. If they locate an outage, they will apply a credit to your account. Last month they credited my account for 7 outages, which worked out to be a savings of $7.00. Now, I jot it down on my calendar, and call my local internet provider each month to have them review my account for the previous 30 days. I save $5-$10 a month this way.

Also, while we are on the topic of internet providers, another way to save and cut back on your monthly bill, is to get your own router. With my own router, I am able to save $5 more a month.

Travel Hack

If you love getting out and exploring new places and traveling, travel hacking may be one the best kept secrets. The premise of travel hacking is to use credit card points made from purchases charged with the card, toward airline flights, hotels and even car rentals. Many credit card companies will offer a large bonus when you sign up for the credit card, and spend a certain amount, typically within the first 3 months of the credit card activation. Once the amount has been charged, the issuer will update your account with travel points. Many people exclusively use these travel points to save on one of the biggest expenses while traveling like airfare, car rental and hotels.

Travel hacking works best if you pay the balance off in full each month as credit card interest rates are typically on the higher side, so it's definitely something to take note of and be sure to not carry a balance forward each month (Moore, 2019).

Calculate your FI Number

At the discovery of financial independence, one of the first tasks is to determine your FI number, or how much you need in order to retire. Many proponents of the F.I.R.E. movement propose the 4 percent rule as a guideline, thus setting a target of at least 25 times the estimated annual living expenses, based upon the Trinity Study. When financial independence is achieved, work in the traditional sense as in a 9-5 or company owner, work is now optional, which allows to retire early earlier than the anticipated age of 59 ½ (Kagan, 2020).

Have you calculated your FI number? Before you can measure your FI number, here are a few things you will need to know. 1) Monthly Expenses, 2) Savings, 3) Earnings; and 4) Investments

Simply put, measure your annual expenditures and multiply by 25. If your operating expenditures are $40,000 a year, you're going to need $1 million to retire. This is the your FI number. This is the number that once you hit it, you are free to walk away from your 9-5. Many wish to go above this number and to pad it to allow for even more room, and more peace of mind. This math in its easiest form, is the magic number to aim for to reach financial independence as soon as possible.

Once we have this number in perspective, then we can really evaluate all the mundane purchases we make over our life. Did I really need to buy the newest and latest Apple iPhone? Did I really need to buy the leather couch instead of fabric one? Did

I really need to buy that new mustang? This is the holy shit moment for many and it puts it all into perspective.

Reverse Engineer your Life

One of the most powerful tools, I have discovered in my own personal journey toward F.I.R.E., is to reverse engineer my life. The concept is to write out the goals of what you want to achieve (e.g., to have 1 million dollars), and from there back into the steps to achieve it, until you get to back to this present day (Reed, 2016).

Let's break it down. By investing in the broad market, you may be able to double your money every 7.5 years with the rule of 72, by not withdrawing funds and reinvesting dividends and capital gains. The rule of 72, is determined by dividing 72 by your rate of return (Pant, 2020). If your FI number is $1M, then you will have to have $500K at least 7.5 years prior and so on. Determine how much you need to have in your investment portfolio and then reverse engineer your finances. Of course, markets fluctuate daily, and this is not a guarantee to return the results desired.

Increase Revenue

Almost 50 percent of Americans anticipate to live paycheck to paycheck this year (Friedman, 2020). Is this number shocking to you? Living paycheck to paycheck is not going to get us to financial independence. In fact, it will probably set us back – and heavily. Many people who are living on the fence of life, struggle to locate funds if an emergency were to rise.

One of the biggest strategies into obtaining financial freedom and independence, is to increase income. Increasing income and revenue can come directly from your main source of income, or it can be through several sources, such as a side hustle, or part time job. When we have more income each month, we can pay off and down debt to increase our savings, which leads to financial independence.

For example, if your post-tax revenue is approximately $6,000 a month, and your monthly expenses are $4,500, the difference of $1,500 is the amount you can use toward savings, investing and paying down debt. The higher your revenue is each month the more you can save and invest.

Pay off Debt

Credit cards and high-interest rate and student loans can set us back quickly, financially speaking. The interest rate on some credit cards can be exorbitant and can impact our ability to save money and to get ahead. As soon as possible pay off debt.

Dave Ramsey, has been teaching people strategies to get out of debt for decades. He discusses the 7 Baby Steps which is great place to begin the journey to financial independence. His strategy in attacking debt is to first set a reserve of $1,000 and then list all debts from smallest to largest. Ramsey then suggests to pay all minimum payments on all debts, except for the smallest one, and to pay as much toward it as possible. Then, when the first debt is paid off in full, to then combine that payment toward debt #2 and so on until all debt has been eliminated (Ramsey, 2020). Many people opt for this strategy as it rapidly provides for momentum in pay off debt. When the smallest debt is paid off, it brings a sigh of relief and we can start to attack the next debt in line.

You can also line up all outstanding debt ranked in order of interest rate. While making minimum payments on all debt, make the largest payment with as much as you can afford, toward the debt with the highest interest rate. Once that debt has been paid off, then move to the next debt that has the next highest rate (Eneriz, 2020). Both of these strategies work well for many, and the objective between these methods is the same – pay off any outstanding debt as soon as possible, with intent.

Refinance your Home

Interest rates are at historical lows, and now may be a good time to refinance your home to obtain a lower interest rate. Call your current mortgage company, and also call around to see who can offer you the best deal. With less interest charged per month, you will have a lower monthly payment. In turn, you could also apply the savings to the principal each month and knock off years on your mortgage obligation.

Build an Emergency Fund

Unexpected events occur, and we have seen this recently with the global pandemic. It's essential to be prepared for job loss, a health emergency, or for a foundation concern in your home. Have an emergency fund of at least 3-6 months in the event a situation occurs. It's better to have peace of mind, and be in a position of low stress when in an emergency. A good place to park this investment is a high-yield savings account, that way you will have immediate access to it should an emergency arise.

Bank Specials

Time to time, many banks offer programs to draw in new members. They may offer a bonus if you sign up and plan to keep money in a savings or investment account. Please be sure to thoroughly read the terms and conditions as it will change from bank to bank. Many people open accounts just to receive the bonus, which is a great way to make extra money. Check out Doctor of Credit, to explore opportunities (Chuck & Charles, 2020).

Start a Side Hustle

There is no shortage of side hustle ideas if you performed a quick google search. It's almost endless. There really is no excuse for not starting and having a side hustle, if your goal is to achieve financial independence, so you can retire early. I have historically had side jobs (hustles) my whole life to get ahead, and I think it's just something that has been a constant part of my life.

Passive income sources that generate wealth when you are sleeping, will have an exponential ability to increase your wealth. Having a side hustle and passive income streams, will open up opportunity for your future to get you out of the rat race sooner. Today is the day to start your side hustle and here are some options:

- Start a blog

- Sell on Amazon or eBay

- Open an Etsy or Shopify store

- Drive for Uber

- Amazon Flex (deliver amazon packages)

- Create training tutorials on your website

- Start a YouTube channel

- Content Creation

- Affiliate Marketing

- Write a book

- Resume Writing Services

- Pet Sitter

- Copywriter

- Virtual Assistant

- Learn to edit videos

- Start a Business

- Teach English Online

- Airbnb

DIY Home Repairs

YouTube is a great resource to learn how to fix things, make small repairs and even learn a new skill. When was the last time you tried to fix your washing machine without calling in a professional? Are there certain tasks you can do yourself without hiring someone? Picking up new skills will alleviate from having to paying someone else to do a job, and you can save money. What is something you would like to learn how to do?

Ask for a Raise

Let's face it, you work hard. You may have been with your current company for quite some time and somedays you may feel overworked and underappreciated. Perhaps the current market conditions have you afraid to ask for a raise, with your current company, for a job well done.

If you have been with your current company for at least a year and the company has not been widely impacted by the current market condition, it's time to ask for a raise. How awesome would it be to have an awesome raise? Here's what you do. First, do some market research on your current position, title, salary with a competing company, even apply for jobs elsewhere to see what you may be offered. You may grossly discover you are underpaid in your current position.

Once you have discovered what your new value is to the company, write down all your current responsibilities and new responsibilities you have either inherited or acquired. Locate your performance metrics on each task and outline how well you have met or exceeded your goal. Create a fabulous PowerPoint presentation to back up your numbers and be ready to provide it to your manager.

Next, set up a time to speak with your direct manager and let them know the topic of the meeting; however, do not have the meeting over email. A Zoom meeting or in-person is preferred as you want to be face-to-face with you direct manager, or the one who can make changes to your salary. Monday's and Fridays' are not good days to have a raise conversation as there is usually too much going on in the office. Pick a Tuesday or even a Thursday. Plan for at least a 3 percent salary increase (Anderson, 2013).

When meeting with your direct manager, have a good attitude and be confident. While the metrics on your PowerPoint should be able to speak for itself; be prepared to negotiate and answer questions from your boss, then sit back and watch them squirm for a bit. They may low ball you, or even decline the raise, but say nothing. You may even need to leave the meeting; this is almost like buying a used car. They will then respond to your request because you have taken the time to do your due diligence, and had the boldness to ask, and had the confidence to be silent during the negotiation. Your boss needs you and honestly wants you stay, however, they have a budget, and the less they pay you in your position, the better their metrics are. You are worth the raise. They will offer, it's okay to negotiate past their first offer. Stick to your original plan and be firm, but don't be a jerk about it. When you get the raise, celebrate, but not where they can see you, and jot it down on your calendar for next year for a similar conversation. Congratulations!

Financial independence with the option to retire early, is created through a series of small accomplishments back-to-back and with momentum, but most importantly take action and take action today. The journey may start off slow, but with persistence, perseverance, determination coupled the right strategy, the day of our financial freedom will approach sooner and sooner.

Chapter Six

Retirement

"How many millionaires do you know who have become wealthy by investing in savings accounts? I rest my case." Robert G Allen

L iving a life that is free from the 9-5, and free from having to produce for others, is a liberating time. It is a highly anticipated time, and is to be thoroughly enjoyed! You have worked hard, invested wisely, and you have built a fantastic nest egg.

At this point in your journey, you have met or exceeded your FI number, have met with your CPA, your family, and those around you who will be impacted by the decision to retire. I am sure they are delighted for you! I am sure there will be a celebratory party in place with all friends and loved ones; well deserved. This has been a long journey!

Immediate life after retirement usually has a time of transition. You may be used to working, saving, investing that when it comes time to retire, you may not be sure what to do, once you have a lot of free time. It may take weeks and months to transition into your new life, so be patient with yourself, and try to go with the flow as much as possible. Eventually you will get used to your new life.

Life after retirement will be what we make of it. It can be either enjoyable or it can be less desirable. Many people choose not to spend idle hours at home, after they retire from work. It has been said numerous times to have a plan. Many early retirees, even in their 30's or 40's need to have an idea on how to spend their time post-retirement. Many early retirees have become out-of-pocket, complacent without a task to do, and have reverted back into full-time work. It's essential to plan in advance of how you will spend your time, so the transition can be fruitful and suit the desired outcome.

During retirement still keep a watchful eye on your investment portfolios. Consult with your tax advisor, and log into your accounts online to observe market trends, growth and loss in your portfolios. Maintain your budget and monitor expenditures so it remains within the scope of your retirement goals. If expenditures are too high one month, make adjustments on the next month.

Remain in connection with your CPA or tax advisor. Have them review your financial matters as often as you feel necessary, so you have a comfort level in the decision you have made to retire early. If you happen to see a dip in the market, it may be worrisome at first, but remember you have reviewed your financial matters backward and forwards, and your FI number has been achieved. The market will constantly fluctuate. Rest assured that you have made a financial choice to retire when the timing is right.

While retirement is a party at first, it's important to keep several things in mind. Retirement will be what you make of it. What are the things you want to accomplish in retirement? Do you want to travel, start a new hobby? Do you wish to volunteer? Many retirees find their time in retirement is pleasurable if they still continue a healthy life, both financially and with a healthy mind and body.

Keep exercise part of your daily regimen. Exercise your mind with books you have wanted to read for a while. Go for a nice walk in the park or a bike ride. Exercise will strengthen the body and mind, act as a stressbuster, and it is the best way to preserve the body and keep it healthy. Keep exercise in retirement as part of your regiment to maintain your growth mindset. Watch what you eat, and maybe even start a garden for fun.

Many early retirees like to travel. Have you made a list of places you would like to see? Perhaps an RV is in order. Take time to explore the country or take a trip abroad. Learn a new culture or language. See the sights. The great thing about retirement is you don't have to rush. You can slow travel, spend quality time at locations of your choosing, and have a blast doing so. Travel is a great way to unwind in early retirement.

One thing that is great about retiring early, is that it allows us to spend more time with friends and family. Relationships are so important to everyday life. Often when we were working many relationships, especially those we have had for many years sometimes get neglected. As we may not have had the time, energy or resources to visit friends as much as we would have liked prior to retiring, now we can make the plans to see and reconnect. Make time for people you may not have seen in a while to see how they are doing! Call up a friend and schedule a lunch meeting. Once we are retired, we realize the value of close friendships.

During retirement, keep your growth mindset intact. Is there a certain skill you would like to learn? Is there a new hobby you'd like to explore? Take a course, or join a class to learn something new! Many retirees enjoy learning a new language, volunteering, or taking a photography course.

Reaching the goal of being financially independent and retiring early is outstanding. You have been incredibly diligent, worked hard, invested wisely, and you are now able to enjoy the fruit of your labor. You are free to spend your time how and when you want. Congratulations. Enjoy retirement! The opportunity you have sought, for perhaps decades or longer, has finally been achieved.

Conclusion

F inancial Independence, Retire Early is a movement dedicated to a program of extraordinary reserve funds that allows proponents to resign far before customary and standard retirement plans would permit. By devoting up to 70% of pay to investments, adherents of the movement may, within the end of the day, have the decision to retire from their occupations and live exclusively off little withdrawals from their portfolio's decades before the regular retirement age of 65. People who strive for F.I.R.E., retire much earlier than 65, usually in their 40's, 30's, and sometimes even in their 20's.

The financial independence, retire early movement, was born in the United States, consists of three stages. First of all, you have to learn to save. And for that, no secret: you have to reduce your lifestyle. It is indeed easier to limit your expenses than to increase your resources. The second step is to go through your account statements to eliminate all unnecessary fees and set a tight budget. Many followers put aside all their free time to save up and invest 70% of their income. Last crucial rule: the money saved must be invested wisely in investments, stocks or real estate, in order to be able to live on savings and investments later. The meaning of financial independence or financial freedom can be summed up in one sentence: living off your income without having to work for a salary.

Resources

Adeney, P. (Mr. Money Mustache). *Mr. Money Mustache Blog*. https://www.mrmoneymustache.com/

(2018). *Pete Adeney (Mr. Money Mustache) – Full Talk at WDS 2016* [Video]. https://www.youtube.com/watch?v=8BDWih309 wc&t=1s

Adcock, S. (2020, June 2). Millionaire who saved 70% of his income and retired at 35: "We should all live by these 6 basic principles." *CNBC*. https://www.cnbc.com/2020/05/31/early-retirement-millionaire-saved-70-percent-of-income-lives-by-basic-money-rules.html

American Psychological Association. (2020). *Marriage and Divorce*. https://www.apa.org/topics/divorce/

Anderson, K. (2013, April 23). The absolute best day to ask for a raise. *MintLife Blog*. https://mint.intuit.com/blog/how-to/the-absolute-best-day-to-ask-for-a-raise-0413/

Chuck, & Charles, W. (2020, December 10). *Bank Account & Credit Card Bonuses*. Doctor of Credit. https://www.doctorofc redit.com/

Cointelegraph. (2017, December 5). What is cryptocurrency? *Cointelegraph*. https://cointelegraph.com/bitcoin-for-beginne rs/what-are-cryptocurrencies

CryptoCurrencyFacts. (2020). *Cryptocurrency Basics Archives*. https://cryptocurrencyfacts.com/section/cryptocurrency-basics/

Dweck, C. (2016). *Mindset: The New Psychology of Success*. Random House.

Eneriz, A. (2020, August 29). Debt avalanche vs. debt snowball: What's the difference? *Investopedia*. https://www.investopedia.com/articles/personal-finance/080716/debt-avalanche-vs-debt-snowball-which-best-you.asp

FIRECalc. (2020). *FIRECalc: How Long Will Your Money Last?* https://www.firecalc.com/

Fleming, J., & Ledogar, R. J. (2008). Resilience, an evolving concept: A review of literature relevant to Aboriginal research. *Pimatisiwin*. https://www.ncbi.nlm.nih.gov/pmc/articles/PMC2956753/

Friedman, Z. (2020, February 19). 49% of Americans expect to live paycheck to paycheck this year. *Forbes*. https://www.forbes.com/sites/zackfriedman/2020/02/19/financial-survey-debt-loans-credit/

Gold Price. (2020). *Gold Price*. https://goldprice.org/

Graham, S. (2018). *Graham Stephan* [YouTube channel]. https://www.youtube.com/channel/UCV6KDgJskWaEckne5aPA0aQ

Hatfield, H. (2020). Shopping spree, or addiction? *WebMD*. https://www.webmd.com/mental-health/addiction/features/shopping-spree-addiction

Hogan, C. What is the F.I.R.E. movement? *DaveRamsey.com*. https://www.daveramsey.com/blog/what-is-the-fire-movement

Holmes-Rahe Stress Inventory. (2020, April 22). *The American Institute of Stress*. https://www.stress.org/holmes-rahe-stress-inventory

How to invest in real estate? *RealEstateForAll.info*. https://ww
w.realestateforall.info/how-to-invest-in-real-estate/

Jobs, S. (2016). A quote by Steve Jobs.
Goodreads. https://www.goodreads.com/quotes/629613-peopl
e-think-focus-means-saying-yes-to-the-thing-you-ve

Kagan, J. (2020, August 28). Four percent rule. *Investopedia*.
https://www.investopedia.com/terms/f/four-percent-rule.asp

Kagan, J. (2020, November 23). 401(k) contribution limits for
2020 vs. 2021. *Investopedia*. https://www.investopedia.com/re
tirement/401k-contribution-limits/

Kiyosaki, R. T., & Lechter, S. L. (1997). *Rich Dad, Poor Dad*.
Warner Books.

Lin, J. T., Bumcrot, C., Ulicny, T., Mottola, G., Walsh, G., Ganem,
R., ... Zepp, P. (2019, June). The state of U.S. financial capability:
The 2018 National Financial Capability Study. *FINRA Foundation*. https://www.usfinancialcapability.org/downloads/NFCS_
2018_Report_Natl_Findings.pdf

Loudenback, T. (2019, May 28). Experts say your office 401(k)
is the best place to start investing. Here's how it works. *Business
Insider*.
https://www.businessinsider.in/experts-say-your-office-401k-i
s-the-best-place-to-start-investing-heres-how-it-works-/artic
leshow/69550383.cms

Loudenback, T. (2019, November 13). How to retire early so you
can work, travel, and relax on your own schedule. *Business Insider*. https://www.businessinsider.com/personal-finance/how
-to-retire-early-steps-for-early-retirement

Maraboli, S. (2019, August 19). Home. *Fearless Motivation –
Motivational Videos & Music*. https://www.fearlessmotivation
.com/

Maroon, J. (2020, September 12). *Financial Freedom Archives.* Journey to Financial Independence. https://jotofi.com/tag/financial-freedom/

Nordstrom, D. S., & T. (2018, March 8). 10 shocking workplace stats you need to know. *Forbes.* https://www.forbes.com/sites/davidsturt/2018/03/08/10-shocking-workplace-stats-you-need-to-know/

Online, F. E. (2018, June 4). Stock market investment: 10 things you must know before investing in stock markets. *The Financial Express.* https://www.financialexpress.com/money/stock-market-investment-10-things-you-must-know-before-investing-in-stock-markets/1192422/

Pant, P. (2020). How the rule of 72 can help double your money. *The Balance.* https://www.thebalance.com/what-is-the-rule-of-72-how-can-it-help-you-double-your-money-453756

Physician, W. S. (2019, September 26). VTSAX review: Invest in the largest mutual fund in the world. *The Wall Street Physician.* https://www.wallstreetphysician.com/vtsax-review/

Ramsey, D. *Dave Ramsey's 7 Baby Steps. DaveRamsey.com.* https://www.daveramsey.com/dave-ramsey-7-baby-steps/

Reed, K. (2016, June 18). How to reverse engineer your life – featuring Gary Vee. *Medium.* https://medium.com/@kylereed/how-to-reverse-engineer-your-life-featuring-gary-vee-f0b02c65de8a

Schneider, O. (2020, June 18). 6 ways to trim your budget, not your lifestyle. *DontPayFull.* https://www.dontpayfull.com/blog/6-ways-to-trim-your-budget-not-your-lifestyle

Sethi, R. (2020, December 2). How to build a Roth conversion ladder. *I Will Teach You To Be Rich.* https://www.iwillteachyoutoberich.com/blog/roth-conversion-ladder/

Shahid, S. (2020, November 12). Please enable cookies. *Stack-Path*. https://www.cloudways.com/blog/trending-products-to-sell/

Team, T. R. (2020, June 22). How ironclad is the one percent rule in real estate investing? *Learn Real Estate Investing*. https://learn.roofstock.com/blog/the-one-percent-rule-in-real-estate-investing-how-ironclad-is-it

Uppaluri, V. S. (2020). *Morningstar, Inc.* Morningstar. https://www.morningstar.com/funds/xnas/vtsax/quote

What are the risks of trading cryptocurrencies? *CMC Markets*. https://www.cmcmarkets.com/en/learn-cryptocurrencies/what-are-the-risks

Wikimedia Foundation. (2020, November 10). Main page. *Wikipedia*. https://en.wikipedia.org/wiki/Financial_independence

Wikimedia Foundation. (2020, November 11). FIRE movement. *Wikipedia*. https://en.wikipedia.org/wiki/FIRE_movement

Wikimedia Foundation. (2020, November 29). Trinity study. *Wikipedia*. https://en.wikipedia.org/wiki/Trinity_study

Xu, J., Murphy, S. L., Kochanek, K. D., & Arias, E. (2020, January 30). Products – Data Briefs – Number 355 – January 2020. *Centers for Disease Control and Prevention*. https://www.cdc.gov/nchs/products/databriefs/db355.htm

www.ingramcontent.com/pod-product-compliance
Lightning Source LLC
Chambersburg PA
CBHW071438210326
41597CB00020B/3855